"You've got to think of him. The way he was. The way he'd cycle round Dublin in his pin-striped suit, with ten thousand pounds on his head. Why hide, he'd say, when that's what they expect. And he never did what anyone expected. Some people are what the times demanded. . . ."

MICHAEL COLLINS

What makes a man lead? What makes a man love? What makes a man kill? What makes a man willing to die? What makes a man the kind of man they call a hero?

NEIL JORDAN is an award-winning writer and internationally celebrated film director. He is the author of *Night in Tunisia*, a collection of stories, and three previous novels, *The Past*, *The Dream of a Beast*, and *Sunrise with Seamonster*. His films include *The Company of Wolves*, *Mona Lisa*, and *The Crying Game*, which won an Academy Award for Best Screenplay in 1993. His last film was *Interview with the Vampire*. He makes his home in Dublin, Ireland.

Michael
COLLINS

Neil Jordan

SCREENPLAY AND FILM DIARY

A PLUME BOOK

PLUME
Published by the Penguin Group
Penguin Books USA Inc., 375 Hudson Street,
New York, New York 10014, U.S.A.
Penguin Books Ltd, 27 Wrights Lane,
London W8 5TZ, England
Penguin Books Australia Ltd, Ringwood,
Victoria, Australia
Penguin Books Canada Ltd, 10 Alcorn Avenue,
Toronto, Ontario, Canada M4V 3B2
Penguin Books (N.Z.) Ltd, 182–190 Wairau Road,
Auckland 10, New Zealand

Penguin Books Ltd, Registered Offices:
Harmondsworth, Middlesex, England

First published by Plume, an imprint of Dutton Signet,
a division of Penguin Books USA Inc.

First Printing, September, 1996
10 9 8 7 6 5 4 3 2 1

ISBN 0-452-27686-1
CIP data is available.

Printed in the United States of America
Set in Meridien
Designed by Stanley S. Drate/Folio Graphics Co. Inc.

CONTENTS

FILM DIARY

It was October 1982. My first film, *Angel*, had just been released. I was checking the proofs of a novel, *The Past*, about to be published by Jonathan Cape. I lived in a beautiful oak-lined flat in Fitzwilliam Square, Dublin. The film I had made, though it had no commercial success whatsoever, caused enough waves of comment to compensate. In Ireland I was accused of misusing public funds, portraying the Irish as irrational and prone to atavistic violence, reinforcing colonial stereotypes, etc. In England the film was inordinately praised, which made them even more suspicious here. My writer friends deplored the fact that I had abandoned literature for movies, the film community deplored the fact that I, a writer, had the presumption to make a film. All in all an interesting time.

David Puttnam had sent me a novel called *Cal*, by Bernard McLaverty, to see was I interested in making a film about it. The story was about a young Derry boy who gets involved in the murder of a policeman and then has a guilt-ridden relationship with his widow. It was too guilt-ridden altogether for my taste. I wrote a letter suggesting that the hero's guilt be salved by the discovery that the widow had always hated the policeman and that far from being her doom, the boy is her redeemer. She can't thank him enough and everything ends happily. I wasn't too surprised when I got no reply

What I did get was a letter asking what I knew about Michael Collins. And the answer, when I asked myself, was very little. A vague impression of a figure in green khaki uniform, something to do with the Civil War and the Fine Gael party. (For those who don't know, one's parents, in my generation were either Fianna Fail or Fine Gael—the two political parties that emerged from the Civil War that grew out of the War of Independence.) But I went to the bookshops and bought a biography of the man—*The Big Fella,* by Frank O'Connor. And while the book was a good one, it did not entirely attract me to the character.

This was 1982, and events in the North of Ireland had entered their bleakest phase. My wife's aunt had been killed by a bomb in Dublin city centre some years before. We had returned from London on the ferry for the funeral and every passenger was an Irish emigrant coming back to bury an aunt, sister, mother or father. I can still remember a huge, straw-haired Dublin woman cursing the country that had sent her jobless to England twenty years before only to draw her back to identify the bunch of remains that had once been her father. The fact that nobody knew who had placed the bomb seemed irrelevant at the time. It was part of the depressing pall of violence that had smothered North and was now threatening to spread down South. And the present masters of this violence were, it seemed, the Provisional IRA, the inheritors of the mantle of the old IRA, for which Collins had written the rulebook.

Over the years my perceptions were to change, as were perceptions in general about that particular bomb which brought me home. To this day it has never been investigated, despite decades of pressure by the relatives who were on that ferry.

One thing did strike me immediately though, when I read the O'Connor book. Through this single character, Michael Collins, one could tell the story of the most pivotal period in Irish history. He was born in West Cork in 1890, of small-farming background, and emigrated to England at an early age where began his interest in Irish Republicanism. He fought in the GPO in the 1916 Rising; became the mastermind of the War of Independence with Britain that followed. It was he who invented most of the strategies of what became known as guerrilla warfare (and was studied by figures as far apart as Mao Tse Tung in China and Yitzhak Shamir in Israel). When the Truce was declared, he was part of the team that negotiated the Treaty with Britain—and was thus in some way responsible for the partition of Ireland, North and South. He became a minister in the new government, Commander-in-Chief of the Free State Army, then acting head of the Provisional Government. And he was shot during the Civil War in West Cork, his homeland, in 1922. Whatever one's attitude towards this period of Irish history, towards the Republican movement, the Treaty and partition of the country, the Civil War—all the contradictions of the period could be convyed through his story. There was potential for a drama here that was huge in its scale, sulphurous of its implications and yet intimate in scope.

So I said yes to David Puttnam, and the contracts followed—with Warner Brothers, which was exciting since I'd never had any contact with a large studio before. And I began seriously to research the man. The biographies were an odd lot. *Michael Collins and The Making Of a New Ireland,* by his friend Piaras Beaslai was essentially a work of hagiography. Written in the thirties, and in the alarmingly heroic mode of those times, it portrayed a mythic figure in the mould of Cuchulain, who combined military prowess, political integrity, and an odd quality which we would now define as charisma. Another, by Rex Taylor, an Englishman who became fascinated by Collins across the divide of the

Irish Sea. And a third, by a New Zealand woman, Margery Forester, who seems to have become gradually obsessed with the man, from no initial knowledge or acquaintance with Irish history whatsoever. Put these together with Frank O'Connor, who fought against Collins during the Civil War, but became so fascinated by him that he wrote what is still probably the best biography, and one can see the peculiar attraction of the man. A certain charisma, across decades and from beyond the grave seems to draw all sorts of people towards him.

Charisma, thought, is a difficult quality to convey in writing: 'He entered the drawing-room with great charisma.' No great help to an actor either. And at first—for the reasons cited above—I was neither seduced nor drawn by the possibility of this charisma. I wrote a script that was dispassionate in its perspectives, fiercely accurate to the history and saw the central character heading towards a doom that was inevitable, given his beliefs and obsessions—nationalism and the use of violence for political ends.

I showed the script to several people, among them Stephen Woolley, Chris Menges and Liam Neeson. Stephen was at the time producing what was to be the first of our many collaborations—*The Company of Wolves* (based on the short story by Angela Carter). Chris had recently photographed my first feature, *Angel*. And Liam had just appeared in his first film role in *Excalibur*, a film on which I had worked as creative consultant to its director, John Boorman. I said to Liam that if I ever got to make the film I would like him to play the part of Collins.

The draft was to be the first of many. David, who is a wise and circumspect reader of such things, felt it lacked a committed sense of the central character and, more important or more disturbingly, lacked an identifiable villain. Now this villain can only be the British—government, Empire, security forces, or a combination of all three. For Irish writers, struggling with the complexity of their history, this is always a problem. For us the divisions within the island are as fascinating as those across the Irish Sea. The wider world, though, wants to see it in more simplistic terms.

I've always found that the time I take to write a script is in inverse proportion to the time it takes a studio to read it. I churned out another draft and while waiting for a reply, found I was able to finish another film, *The Company of Wolves*. Thus I established a rhythm which would sustain me over the next twelve years. I would write a draft, do my best to get it made, then, while awaiting a reply, go and make another film. With *The Company of Wolves* made and released, I returned to the Collins project, addressed the readers' and producers' notes, and in the great silence that followed, embarked on another film, *Mona Lisa*.

After *Mona Lisa* came one of those seismic power-shifts that happen every now and then in Hollywood. David Puttnam took over the running at Columbia Studios and terminated his agreement with Warners. Mark Rosenburg, the head of production at Warners, wanted to keep the Collins project with his studio, so I embarked upon another rewrite for him. Meanwhile David, whose interest in the project was genuine and never wavered, had come across another script on Collins and put it into production with Michael Cimino as director. I was back in Ireland, and in a fit of madness or desperation embarked on my first quasi-Hollywood project—*High Spirits*. I was about to get my fingers burned.

Cimino's film eventually collapsed before principal photography. Kevin Costner, whose *Dances With Wolves* had be-

come an enormous success, then took up the reins. I
resigned myself to seeing somebody else's version of the
story on the screen, made two other films, and always returned in between to what had now become a private ob-
session with the Collins project.

In 1992 I made *The Crying Game* which became a huge
hit, as much to my surprise as anyone else's. It dealt with
the contemporary IRA, and with political violence, among
a host of other things. What irritated a lot of critics in Britain was the fact that it refused to make *a priori* judgements
on its central character, played by Stephen Rea. He was not
presented as a psychopath or a cold-blooded terrorist, but
as a rational human being. His actions, however dreadful
in themselves, were not motivated by pathology but by a
political point of view, which itself was amenable to
change. Whether this was a response to a change in my
thinking, or some internal response to the political climate
on this island is hard to gauge. Despite the popular percep-
tion of movies as machines for the manipulation and or
distortion of people's emotions, a screenplay, to be any
good, has to discover its own internal life. A character has
to tell the author what it wants to do, rather than vice-
versa. And, equally, a story has to tell the film where it
wants to go. With *The Crying Game,* I wanted to see where
this central character, informed by a political perspective
which is as old as this island itself, as the conflict itself,
could go; confronted with an enemy that was a human
being rather than a cipher, with the whole maelstrom of
the contemporary wider world—issues of race, of gender,
of a wider moral responsibility than the narrow confines of
South Armagh—how would he be changed?

The film was a commercial success and won me an
Oscar. I went on to make another film, this time for David

Geffen and Warner Brothers—*Interview with the Vampire,* which was for me a return to the gothic world I found I loved so much in *The Company of Wolves.* And after the release of that film, Warners and David asked me what I wanted to do next. I reminded them of the Collins project, which had been gathering dust in their vaults. And miraculously, for the first time in twelve years, there seemed a real possibility of my making it.

I returned to my house in Dublin and dragged out the huge pile of drafts I had written. What was new, of course, in the intervening years was the Peace Process. For the first time, the guns were silent in the North and looked like remaining silent. And as I read through the drafts, I could see how the character was changing. From the dispassionate, rather dry perspective of the first draft, Collins began progressively to breathe with life. That intangible quality, charisma, had crept in almost without my realising. But I saw that to make the film would be to confront the issue of the uses of political violence within Irish politics head on. And I realised the only possible perspective the film could take was the perspective of the participants themselves. Michael Collins, Éamon de Valera, Harry Boland—from the years 1916 to 1922—to show them in all their confusion, divisions, hopes and disillusions.

Collins didn't invent guerrilla warfare. He didn't introduce the gun into Irish politics. That was a centuries-old tradition. What he did was to take the traditional pieties of Irish Nationalism and turn them into realistic aims. What he did was to say, if this is our aim, independence from Britain, here is how it can be practically achieved. He masterminded a kind of war that was brutal, as all wars are, but more intimate than most. And his uniqueness in Irish history is the fact that having achieved what he could with these tactics, he then tried to put a halt to them. The fact that he was undone in the end by the traditional Irish nationalistic pieties—the ideal of the pure and pristine republic—is what makes him a genuinely tragic figure.

So we got a green light for the film. Then we embarked on a process which was eerie in the way a whole series of contemporary events parallelled the ones in the past we were filming.

Wednesday 21st December 1994

I do a series of Irish interviews for *Interviews With the Vampire*. I love this move, love the book, by Anne Rice, it was based on, but am very aware that it is less a horror movie than a gothic passion play. When your central characters cannot die, the thrills and terrors of traditional horror take a back seat. You will never fear for them, though you may fear them. Thus the film, though a large hit, is not to everybody's taste. Horror movies are rarely to everyone's taste. The aficionados are fierce in their loyalty, their fidelity and knowledge of the genre. The general public go to see it more like a freak show.

I do Irish press all day, which is the only kind that makes me nervous. Because they know where you come from, know your background, knew you when you had no arse to your trousers, so to speak.

A dinner party at a friend's, Monica Frawley's. Tom Murphy is there, the playwright. Just published his first novel which I read and which is very good. He is as anguished as ever and his anguish makes him even more attractive. Sees life solely through emotional loss and turmoil. Everyone drinks too much, including me, and I know I'm home.

Thursday 22nd December

Jean Kennedy Smith, the American Ambassador to Dublin has a dinner party at her residence in the Phoenix Park. Was this the viceroy's lodge, I wonder, or is that Aras an Uachtaran where the President sits. She manages to make the world of power and diplomacy seems comfortable. Jean asks me can she play a part in the film. Any part, no matter how small. Tells me she was once in a Woody Allen film but ended up on the cutting-room floor. I promise to try and think of something.

Friday 23rd December—Tuesday 3rd of January 1995

Christmas at home in Dalkey. All the family there, Anna, Sarah, Brenda, Daniel and Dashiel, Ursula (minus Michael), Jean; Ben drops by, and Vivienne. I took to going skiing after Christmas to avoid the debilitation of all the piss-ups leading to New Years. Don't manage it this year.

Thursday 5th January

I begin rewriting the Collins script. I have to pull all the numerous drafts from every conceivable corner of the office. There are more than a dozen. I can never work out whether the amount of time spent on a project helps it or not. This one has gone through so many hands, so many notes from so many executives, potential producers, that it seems very far away from me now. Some scripts, like *The Butcher Boy,* I write in almost one continuous sitting. Others, like *The Crying Game,* sit around for years, fermenting like a vintage wine—or some plonk from a bad year. But in general the final thing is written in one sustained burst. I suppose I have to write it with something like the momentum with which one experiences it on the screen, where the ideas come to me with a visceral, subconscious excitement and the emotional and the rational logic are all mixed up.

This one has a specific problem. When Stephen Rea plays the character of Fergus in *The Crying Game,* he plays a fictional character. So one confuses the actor with the character, which has no existence outside of him. But when Rod Steiger, say, plays Napoleon one knows that the character, Napoleon, has had a very firm existence in no way dependent on Rod Steiger. The actor is emphatically not the character. And this fact hampers the characterisation in all sort of unseen ways. Damn these Moscow winters. Historical reality is both a stimulus and a snare.

With the Collins script this is an added burden since the story is so intimately known by the whole country. And in many ways the issues are still current. Partition, the uses of political violence, the attempt to create peace out of war, in effect to decommission an army.

I get to work anyway and make two basic decisions. One, not to take the story to London. The whole issue of the Treaty negotiations with Britain, the tortuous experience of the Irish delegation with the British cabinet, the fact that Sir James Craig, leader of the Ulster Unionists, had in essence set up the Northern state, the confusion of instruction from de Valera, the way the arguments back home about the Treaty concentrated on the symbolic issue of the oath of allegiance to Britain rather than the much more crucial issue of partition—all of these are so complex that they would need another movie all to themselves. Rather like *Godfather 2*. I resolve to tell this part of the story purely in terms of our Irish characters. In other words, de Valera sends Collins to London to negotiate. Collins protests he is unfit for the job. Goes under duress. While there, discovers what de Valera knew all along: that any peace must involve an unpalatable compromise. Comes back, having brought back the best he could—which he regards as a basis upon which they can build a future republic. And de Valera, for reasons that are still obscure, rejects it. Whether de Valera set him up, or genuinely thought he, being the military hard man, could have done a better job, remains a mystery. And becomes the essential drama. This means Lady Lavery (British socialite and reputedly Collins's lover) will not make it into the film. And the popular romantic image of Collins as an Irish Don Juan among the English upper classes won't make it either. I don't say it didn't happen. But since we don't take him to London, we don't see it.

The other decision is to reduce the cast of characters. There are so many, drifting through various parts of the story that the audience would end up in utter confusion. Joe O'Reilly, who was Collins's devoted fellow-traveller through all these years didn't accompany him on his last trip. Emmet Dalton did. But to bring in somebody we have never met in the last chapter would be ludicrous. So I merge the characters of Joe and Emmet Dalton. Also, the various detectives who collaborated with him from Dublin Castle—Ned Broy, David Nelligan et al,—will have to be merged into one. And the climactic night on the eve of Bloody Sunday in November 1920, when three Volunteers are lifted in Vaughan's Hotel and done to death in the Castle, poses a problem. This is the first time we meet them, and their deaths mean nothing. So I merge them with the character of Ned Broy. Ned Broy is lifted, done to death in the Castle. Now, in fact, Ned Broy lived into old age, established the police-force in the new Free State and later ran the Broy Harriers—which was to become the scourge of the Republican movement after the Civil War. I realise this is taking the single greatest historical licence in the screenplay. I wonder should I change his name to an entirely fictional one. But in his name is a marvellous pun—when Soames, the leader of the Cairo gang (the group of English secret service men who come to Dublin at the height of the Black and Tan war to eliminate Collins, and so called because they would meet in the Cairo café in Dublin) arrives he constantly calls him 'Boy'. Thank you, Boy, that will be all. It's Broy, sir, Broy. Yes, Broy. So I have no alternative but to call him Broy. And I tell myself that Shakespeare did far worse with Holinshed.

So the story basically falls into two parts. The first, from 1916 to the announcement of the Truce, where our characters with a very definable set of aims and ideals foment the War of Independence with whatever means available to them. Bloody, quite horrific, but whatever we think about their means, we can understand their aims. The second, from the Truce to Collins's death in 1922, where the machine they have created destroys them one by one, under pressure of the complexities of the relationships within this island and of the intractable way in which the British saw their empire. The story to be told from the point of view of the characters themselves. Sharing their aims, their perspectives and ultimately their confusions.

The last issue I suppose is Collins's death. And having

read all of the material available on it and taking into account the reticence that prevailed after the Civil War, where people were unwilling to discuss the events in detail, there are two solid facts I can come up with. One, that he was shot by the West Cork IRA, in an ambush that was militarily justifiable, given there was a Civil War. Two, that some meeting, some attempt at revolution was in the air. De Valera, Liam Lynch and what remained of the Republican leadership were meeting in a farmhouse at Beal na mBlath on the morning of the day Collins was killed. Power had passed from de Valera's hands since the war broke out. And Collins was shot driving through that small, inconsequential Valley. I think that the surmise that Collins was attempting a meeting and was killed in the course of that attempt is a reasonable one—perhaps the only reasonable one. Otherwise how can one explain his presence there? The Irregulars, as Collins called them, had been driven from the rest of the country, from Dublin, Cork and Limerick. Bands of them were drifting from Cork city towards West Cork, and from Limerick in the same direction. For a military strategist as good as he was to travel there was either an attempt at suicide or an attempt at some kind of resolution. So I construct a miniature drama on the eve of his death in the absence of any explanation of these mysteries. A meeting with a young Republican outside a West Cork pub, who asks him has he a message for Dev. Collins delivers him an impassioned one. How Harry Boland's death was enough. How Dev was always his chief. How he would have followed him to hell if he'd asked him. How maybe he did. But it's not worth fighting for any more. You tell him that.

Collins returns to the pub. The kid wanders back into a hayrick. There we see de Valera, moved to tears by Collins's words. So I take it you heard, the kid says. Have you any reply? De Valera wanders off into the night, unable to speak. The kid, however, returns to the pub. Meets Collins. And lies to him. Dev says he'll meet you tomorrow. Beal na mBlath, there's a farmhouse to the left on the Bandon side. Around twelve.

The next morning Collins travels to this apparent meeting and instead meets his death.

This scene makes three assumptions. One, that some meeting was mooted. Two, that de Valera was basically powerless at the time. Three, that Collins was shot by the West Cork IRA. All three I believe are true. The scene is an extrapolation from these assumptions. A surmise. A fiction, based on historical surmise, which is all one can do given the murky nature of the known facts. It says something, I hope, about the broader truth and the state the protagonists found themselves in.

Anyway, as always, the only thing that will stimulate me to finish a script is a realistic prospect of it being made. This is at last the case and the prospect, as Dr Johnson might have said, concentrates the mind wonderfully. It comes to life again and is finished in a couple of weeks.

Monday 9th January

In London doing press for my novel. *Sunrise with Seamonster.* The title taken from the strange Turner painting, *Sunrise with Sea Monsters,* in the Tate. It has been used before, I find out, for a book of travel writings by Paul Theroux, little known in England but popular in America. So I have to change the title in America—to *Nightlines.* Which is the title of a book of short stories by John McGahern, little known in America but popular here.

It is the first novel I have written for eight years. The intervening years have been spent making films of various kinds, dealing with the apparent vagaries of that behemoth, the movie business. Over those eight years, though, the business of publishing seems to have become equally monstrous. Random House seems to have taken over most of the small publishers in Britain. During the course of the publication of this book my editors change three times. This makes the merry-go-around of executive power that happens in movie companies seem positively sedate, almost Victorian. Anyway. Everyone I get to deal with seems very sweet and supportive, the only problem being that they are gone the next week.

I had written two books before I made a film. As soon as I made one film, though, my fiction was reviewed as the work of a film-maker. We live in a world of brand names, I suppose. Heinz makes beans, Neil Jordan makes films and Andy Warhol is the guy who said that in the future everyone will be famous for fifteen minutes. And it is a handy situation for critics. Those who like the book can say he should never have started making films, those who dislike it can say he never should have stopped.

I give a reading in a Waterstone's bookshop in North London and am immediately taken back into that world, the one I started in. A world of cigarette ash, crumpled manuscripts, poetry readings. Pat McCabe is there, and Dermot Healy. I'm taken back to readings in Belfast, years ago. The Northern poets would turn out in mass for any visiting writer. John Hewitt, Michael Longley, Paul Muldoon, James Simmons, Edna Longley. Nothing if not circumspect. The words received in coded silence. Then John

Hewitt approaches, tells me that as I read my prose he has been scanning it. The rhythms were invariably in iambic pentameter. I am about to take this as a compliment when he asks do I consider this appropriate for prose . . . ?

I feel oddly exposed and naked reading for this attentive audience. The presence of my dead father behind this tortuous story that I wrote—I feel almost embarrassed about the sense of personal revelation. And don't want to be questioned about it. And remember that I always felt that way. Maybe I took up making films to get a new suit, a more complete disguise.

Spend the night drinking with Pat and Dermot in my flat. Severe dissolution of the senses which leads to great conversation and a very bad hangover.

Wednesday 11th January

Fly to Belfast for more interviews and a reading at the Queen's Theatre. And I'm reminded of those readings years ago, after which the assembled literati would repair to a portacabin of a bar that had been bombed, the entrance surrounded by a steel cage where one was frisked by a tough stocky guy in an anorak. The literary ethos then was one of endurance, of the space that writing could carve for itself in the midst of all these sectarian definitions. Which had its own nobility. But now it is a different city. Peace has brought gentrification, mobility, restaurants, a heady kind of freedom. But there are no poets at the reading.

Thursday 12th January

There is something wrong with the train, so we are driven to Dublin by a wee Protestant driver who becomes more nervous the further south he goes. A nice old man, tiny, with greying hair and few words. As we drive through Dublin city out to Dalkey I can feel his sense of disorientation turn into fear. How Dalkey with its long lawns and its private villas could hold terrors for anyone is beyond me. But the poor man is seriously disturbed and I realise he has probably never ventured into what they call the Free State before. I give him as accurate directions as I can as to how to get out of this ghetto, and wish him well.

That night there is a launch for the novel in the Dublin bookstore in Grafton Street. Seamus Heaney is there and Jean Kennedy Smith among others. I have found a small part for Jean to play and tell her that. Any journalists there who should be talking to me about the book just want to ask about the Collins film. Who's in it, who's playing de Valera, etc. Alarming, but a taste of what's to come. The subject in Ireland sets a fever running. A combination of things—the Peace Process, the gap of time, the sense that Collins always represented lost possibilities. And I suppose the memory this generation has of their grandparents.

Monday 16th January

Opening of *Interview with the Vampire* in Dublin. Tom Cruise comes over, bless his heart. He promised to do so months ago, and I had always thought circumstances would intervene. But here he is, causing a sensation in O'Connell Street. Police holding back crowds, as if the Beatles had returned. He makes his way through a quite terrifying line and finds time to talk to everybody. All I know is I couldn't do it.

A party afterwards in Dublin Castle. Liam Neeson turns

up. Michael D. Higgins and a group of British MPs who
have come to see how the tax-breaks have worked for the
Irish film industry. James Callaghan and a Labour spokes-
man for defence among them. I talk to him for a while and
get the impression they found the film quite loathsome.
Maybe they don't want this kind of activity on their shores
after all. When you have Shakespeare, why do you need
movies?

Tuesday 17th January

Travel to London the next day for a repetition of the same
event. *Vampire* opening in Leicester Square. A party in San
Lorenzo's in Knightsbridge.

Wednesday 18th January

Give a *Guardian* Lecture at the National Film Theatre with
Stephen Woolley (the film's producer). The audience seem
to genuinely love the film. Though the reviews that are
coming out are quite bitchy. An odd phenomenon is taking
place, which is partly to do with the success of the distribution tactics of the major companies. They make large block-
buster films critic-proof. The success and notoriety of the
film in America almost guarantees it an audience here. And
with that goes the sort of advance press, magazine articles,
television coverage that makes a critic redundant. Whatever they say, people will go to see it. This impotence leads
to a kind of rage. Most evident in Alexander Walker's piece
in the *Evening Standard* which seems to me quite shocking
in its personalised venom. For a small movie with limited

distribution, critics are your only contact with a public. And they use that power quite responsibly. But with a larger film, perspective can go to the wind, I suppose.

Thursday 19th January

Steve (Woolley) and I fly to West Cork where Liam (Neeson) is waiting. We check into the Skibbereen Arms Hotel and go to meet the Collins family. Welcomed at the home of Liam Collins, Michael's nephew, and his wife with old-fashioned rural courtesy. Visit the old farmhouse at Woodfield which has been landscaped quite beautifully into a fitting monument. No museums or interpretative centres here. Just a preserved old burnt-out farmhouse, with a lovely oak tree in the garden and a plaque or two. One gets the impressions of quite severe intelligence here, and of a reticence that has accumulated over the years—a necessary reticence given that neighbours and families would have been so divided by the events of the Civil War.

I have forgotten how tall Liam is and am shocked for a moment. Six-foot-four in his stocking feet. I'll have to angle the camera all the time to get him and Joe O'Reilly in the same frame. Joe was, like most Irishmen, five-foot-nothing. We go to the Four-Alls pub and hear stories of the various directors and actors who passed through here, researching the same film. Michael Cimino, Kevin Costner, even, apparently, John Huston. Kevin Costner we are told turned down the offer of a pint of Guinness for a cup of tea. Liam immediately orders four more pints. Then four more and more again until I'm almost footless.

We go back to the Skibbereen Arms, have dinner and then head for a pub across the way which stays open late.

More pints of Guinness until I turn a bleary eye to the television screen and see Liam on it. It's the first movie he ever did in America, a TV movie where he plays a serial killer. Extraordinary energy and magnetism. That dangerous quality he had when I first saw him on stage, playing Doalty Doran in Brian Friel's *Translations*. I will always remember the way he leaned against the cabin window, while the British officer railed about the retribution the village could expect, then turned nonchalantly and said, Tell him his tents are on fire. And I find a key to the character there—and to a certain secret in the story. The villain and the hero in this piece are merged into one. For the problem always in movies of this type is that the central character often ends up characterless. Goodness is essentially undramatic. Thus, while in *Schindler's List* he gave a superb performance, and should have won an Oscar in my view, the critical plaudits went to Ralph Fiennes, who played a quite conventional caricature of evil. In Michael Collins he can embody both principles. A man with as many gradations within him as there are between black and white, someone who is at times appalled by his own capacity for violent action. And he has the advantage of immutable likeability. He could bury his grandmother in concrete and you would still sympathise with him. I try to explain this, and don't know whether I succeed or not. It's too late and not the time. But I can keep it for later.

Friday 20th January

We wake up that morning and drive to Beal na Blath, the scene of Collins's death. We get lost on the way, as apparently did he, and attempting to find our way in the maze of tiny roads through fields and one-pub villages make me wonder again about the journey. Either every other possible route to Bandon was blocked/blown up, or an attempt at a meeting had been arranged. Eventually we find the place. See the farmhouse where de Valera, Liam Lynch and the Republican leadership met that morning. See Long's pub where Dinny the Dane gave them directions. We walk up to the ambush site and it is nothing spectacular, special only in its air of non-consequence. So his life ends in non-descript absurdity, in an ambush that was almost called off, the possibility of an encounter that never occurred. A metaphor for most relationships on this island.

Travel back to Dublin. Do the *Late, Late Show* with Gay Byrne. For those who don't know, this is the Irish equivalent of Dave Letterman and Jay Leno rolled into one. And it has been running since they have had television in Ireland. I've avoided it for years, because it is the one thing that makes your face known here. As it is, I'm generally confused with Jim Sheridan and complimented for *My Left Foot*, which is fine by me. Actors and rock stars deserve that recognition since they're paid so much. Writers and directors are paid to be anonymous. And halfway through the show I realise that anonymity here for me is gone for ever. The interest in this Collins film is turning it into a national institution. My problem now is how to make a film that won't feel like a national institution.

Tuesday 24th January

Liam Neeson, Natasha Richardson and Tim Pat Coogan come out to Dalkey for dinner. Natasha is pregnant and very beautiful. Liam like a stallion brought to ground. Tim

Pat reminds me of nothing so much as the Citizen in *Ulysses*. Maybe because he has eye trouble and has to wear an eye-patch. He is an extraordinary raconteur, denigrated by some here as a nationalist of the old green type, but I find his conversation refreshing. The fashion since the sixties in Ireland has been for history of the dispassionate, reductive type, labelled revisionism, as if any account of a period is not a revision of the previous account. And what that can't explain is the appeal of personality, nor the psychological complexities of myth, identity and colonial schizophrenia. So Tim Pat steps into the breach. His biography of Collins is remarkable, for one who edited the de Valera/Fianna Fail organ, the *Irish Press,* for many years. His biography of de Valera is even more so, given that relationship. He fills Liam in on a host of details, anecdotes. And I realise that whatever the nature of the finished film, it will open a hornet's nest. So much of the subject matter reeks of sulphur. So it must be worth doing.

Thursday 2nd February

Travel to London with Stephen Woolley (producer) and Redmond Morris (co-producer). We have to meet Roy Button who runs the production end of Warners in England out at Pinewood. There is a large, expensive set to be built, without which I know the film can't be made. O'Connell Street and the GPO are blasted to rubble at the start of the film, in 1916. They are blasted to rubble again towards the end of the film, during the Civil War. If we don't build a huge set which we can wreck and rebuild and wreck again, we can't make the film. The question is how can we justify building that set in Ireland. Labour is more expensive, materials are more expensive, and much of the skilled craft-work will have to be brought in—plasterers, modellers, painters. The industry in Ireland has never sustained a production as large as the one we are planning. And we are trying to make it cheap. I try to argue in indefinables. How the support we will get across the board in Ireland will more than compensate for the added cost. But I can feel I'm not winning.

Friday 3rd February

All day at Pinewood going through the set with Tony Pratt, our production designer. He has built a cardboard model of the set which we try to reduce piece by piece. It becomes like a Lego game. What if this street went there, this building went there? If we combined this scene with that, basically squeezed geography the way in the script I have squeezed history. Tony worked with Cimino on his attempt at the project, which came to grief when the costs of his projected full-scale build of O'Connell Street came in at approximately six million dollars. We decide to look for a site in Dublin where we can use some existing structures. Factory, warehouse complex, something like that.

In the evening I meet Stephen Rea. I originally wrote the script with Liam and Stephen in mind for Collins and Harry Boland. But I have a feeling that the part of the detective Ned Broy would be far more satisfying for Stephen. In addition, he has a part that would conflict, so it might suit him better. We've made three films together and conversations with him are as simple as they can be. Far too intelligent to be fully satisfied by acting, he has spent years committed to the Field Day Company, with Brian Friel,

Seamus Heaney and Seamus Deane, driving it forward often with only his own commitment, to the detriment of what agents would call his acting career. The truth is, too, that the part of Broy needs an actor as subtle as Stephen to make it what it should be. He takes my point, I think, and agrees to play Broy.

Saturday 4th February

Fly to Los Angeles. Stay at the Peninsula Hotel. I always see the city under the fog of jetlag, so never know what I really think about it. When I came here first I was entranced by all the pastel pinks and greens and blues. I spent several years here, made two films and the city did to me what it often does to others. Drives them crazy. I went back to Ireland then and got myself into some semblance of sanity, but over the years I've come to know more people here than I do at home, so it's become an ersatz home. A mental home.

Monday 6th February

Meet with Terry Semel, Bob Daly and David Geffen at Warner Brothers. David, who can cut through executive miasma in a way I've never seen anyone do, has brought the film to this point, where they are actively considering making it. Terry and Bob, who are gentlemen, see it as uncommercial but decide to give it the go-ahead. I am as happy about the project as I've ever been. The next day, though, I discover the catch.

Tuesday 7th February

Meet with Bill Young, Warner's production executive, Stephen (Woolley) and Red (Morris) to go through the budget. What we had asked them for was $25 million, the minimum for which the film can be made. On top of that was the Irish tax break which would give us another ten per cent again. Mine and Stephen's fees were to be the guarantee against any overcost. We have a rather confused meeting with Bill, who always reminds me of my uncle Eamon, where between our understanding and his there seems to be a significant gap. He tells us they have come up with basically what we asked for, but in a different form. Tells us to talk to Jeff Berg, who will fill us in on the details.

We drive round to International Creative Management and meet Jeff, for many years my American agent. Jeff, who is as happy as I was the previous day, shakes my hand congratulates us and explains their proposal in detail. Their understanding apparently was that the $25 million included the Irish tax breaks. Which leaves us approximately two and a half million short. Which budget is to be guaranteed with my own fee. I realise we can't make the film for this and tell Jeff this. I ask him to thank them very kindly, but to explain that the situation isn't possible. I resolve to get on with making another, smaller film, *The Butcher Boy,* based on the novel by Pat McCabe.

Over the next two days David gets on the phone, like a whirling dervish. Telling me I have to make this film, telling Warners I don't know what, but within two days it is back on track and we have the money we need. Take a holiday in Canada to recover from all the drama.

On the way back to Dublin, stop off in New York to begin the casting. Meet Matt Dillon, Billy Baldwin, Aidan

Quinn, Mary-Louise Parker, Dennis Leary, among others. I always love casting sessions. Basically, what better way is there to meet people? Matt Dillon is so passionate about the part of Harry Boland, I feel guilty saying he is such an American icon it might not work. How could I be more Irish? Matt asks me, and I feel like a shabby racist. And he is absolutely right. Because your parents had to emigrate, does that cancel your nationality? I have to think about this one.

Aidan Quinn, though, is quite luminous. Startling blue eyes, a quietness about him that is perfect. I'm not sure how much he wants the part of Harry Boland, however. And as always, meeting American actors, I think the pity is how little real opportunity Hollywood movies give them.

Thursday 23rd February

Back in Dublin. Meet with Chris Menges and Tony Pratt and begin searching for locations. Chris is one of the world's greatest cameraman, and like all of the others he has been lost to direction. He photographed *Angel,* my first film, and I could never get him to work again. But we discussed the Collins film then, and he said if I ever got to make it he would photograph it. I initially asked Philippe Rousselot, with whom I had done three other films, to photograph it. But Philippe too had gone over to direction and was about to direct his own film. And as I was searching desperately through the agents' lists to find a replacement Chris rings up, reminds me of our conversation and says he wants to do it.

So here we are driving round Dublin, finding out how we can make the city even approximate to the one Joyce described in *Dubliners, Portrait of the Artist* and *Ulysses*. And I gradually come to realise it's as big a reconstruction job as Joyce did imaginatively in Paris. The Stalinist rubbish that almost ruined the city in the sixties is one thing. That was halted by recession, but since the economy picked up again, there has been a minimalist invasion. Façades will have to be altered, whole streets put out of action, every lamppost replaced. We will basically have to be given the whole city centre as a set, which is a matter of politics, departmental diplomacy as much as money. The job seems absolutely impossible, but we resolve to keep that a secret. If the scale of what we were trying to do became known, the budget would seem laughably optimistic.

Monday 27th February

An odd phenomenon taking place—an explosion of *Uncle Vanyas*. One which I saw in New York, a film by Louis Malle of a version by David Mamet of a series of rehearsals of the play starring Julianne Moore and Wally Shawn. I saw the film for Julianne Moore, who is a remarkable actress— considering her for the part of Kitty Kiernan. Another, which I see now in Dublin, is a Field Day production starring Stephen Rea. I go to see Stephen in it and once again conclude that I don't understand this play. It has more delayed exits than an Irish wake. The last act alone is a series of interminable and interrupted goodbyes. But I must be wrong, since actors love it and Michael Colgan, the director of the Gate Theatre tells me it is the greatest play ever written. The essential action has taken place years ago, the resolution itself is already in the past and the main event on the stage is the leaving of it. But maybe that is it.

Thursday 2nd February

Have a day-long meeting at Radio Telefis Eireann. I am a member of the Irish Film Board and am on a committee to award a series of grants for short films to be made by Irish filmmakers. The idea seemed a good one, but as always the money is not enough and the enterprise gets caught up in a series of quasi-political arguments. RTE, co-funding the scheme, is accused of buying cheap programming, which may be the case. The unions accuse the scheme of pegging the costs of each film so low that even minimum cannot be paid. Which also may be the case. So from making a commitment of my time and energy, to something that would help emerging directors I find myself in the position of providing cheap programming for a TV station and forcing people to work on subsistence wages. Which may be the case. Where do you start? As they say in Dublin, if you're going there I wouldn't start from here.

Monday 6th March

Jeff Berg calls and says Julia Roberts might be interested in the part of Kitty Kiernan. I say I would love to meet her but am privately worried by the complications a big star would bring to a role like this. I tell Jeff we have no money and he says Julia understands this. The situation is complicated by the fact that Stephen (Woolley) is at some stage in discussions with the agent of another actress, Mary-Louise Parker. I had met her in New York and found her very special, but was worried about her for that particular part. While I was watching her performances on video, the agent had called to say if we didn't make an offer we might lose her, which agents tend to do. I had been putting off a decision and didn't know at what stage things were.

Tuesday 7th March

Fly to Toronto for the funeral of Brenda's mother, Marion Rawn. Marion had been ill for some years, of a stroke and kidney failure. We drive outside Toronto to a small church in a little farming town called Stainer. A strange, simple beauty about the event. Her sons carry the coffin and don't try to hide their grief. It is 40° below outside, so cold they cannot dig a grave.

Friday 10th March

Fly to New York, meet Julia Roberts with Stephen Woolley in the ICM offices in Manhattan. Of all the actresses I have met for the role, she is the one who knows most about it. I didn't realise she had spent so much time in Ireland. She is quite wonderful and as usual some instinct takes over and I offer her the part. She understands about the money, there is no demurring, we shake hands and that is it. There will be objections, I know: anytime you cast a Hollywood star there are. The same happened with Tom Cruise (in *Vampire*). And in some way I feel sorry for the positions they find themselves in. It might seem ludicrous to pity someone who is paid $12 million a film, but in many ways that very fact limits your options terribly. The system needs people who are young, and extraordinary in some physical and emotional way, throws them into this world of movies and forces them to learn to act on the job. But when a film comes up that implies some possibility of serious acting, the world objects. They see a matinée idol and want them to remain that way. Anyway, it's done.

In between times I meet John Turturro. Susie Figgis (casting director) came up with this intriguing idea of casting him as de Valera. He has the hawklike profile and the strange, obsessive abstraction necessary and is obviously a great actor. But after a half an hour of conversation I realise the part is too far from his experience for him to be interested.

Tuesday 21st March

Casting in London with Susie Figgis in the Groucho Club. Susie brings in a rake of comedians to see me. Sean Hughes, Jimeoin, Owen O'Neill. All for the part of Joe O'Reilly. I ask Sean does he really want this part and he says no, he just loves coming into the Groucho at ten in the morning. But the cast is taking shape. Liam (Michael Collins), Aidan Quinn (Harry Boland), Stephen Rea (Ned Broy), Julia Roberts (Kitty Kiernan), Brendan Gleeson (Liam Tobin), Gerry McSorley (Cathal Brugha). The two outstanding parts uncast are Joe O'Reilly and de Valera. Films can be seeded with potential disaster at two stages. One is if the script is compromised or unfinished. The other is if the casting is compromised or sloppily constructed. I've had experience of both and want to get it right this time.

Dinner with Sandy Powell (costume designer) in Dawson Street. Sandy's instincts are far more baroque than this film is. *Interview with the Vampire* suited her perfectly. So I'm worried she mightn't be stimulated by this, which is basically costume of the common people, so to speak. But she is so good that the consistency of what she does even to the minor characters speaks volumes. Anyway, she definitely wants to do it.

Wednesday 29th March

Susie in Dublin again for casting. We begin to populate all the smaller parts. Collins's Squad, Charlie Dalton, Vinnie Byrne et al. Meet a great array of young actors in Dublin. Everyone wants to be in the film, in a role no matter how small. David Gorey, Tom Murphy, David Wilmot form the basis of the Squad. Brendan Gleeson, who played Michael Collins himself in the RTE production of the Treaty, agrees to play Liam Tobin. Sean McGinley will play the dog Smith, head of the Castle detectives. Owen Roe comes on as Arthur Griffith, Paul Bennet as Cosgrove, his daughter as Rosie, Charlie Dalton's young girlfriend who gives Collins the scraps from the wastepaper baskets in the boarding-houses of the Cairo gang.

We are still stuck for de Valera, Soames (the head of the Cairo gang) and Joe O'Reilly. Every Irish actor who has played de Valera has played him as a caricature. And I suppose he is such a familiar figure to us that an Irish actor can't resist that. So I decide not to go down that route. Alan Rickman comes to mind and we agree to offer it to him. He could look like him and might have the gravitas to pull it off. Then comes the matter of the English characters, chief among them Soames, the character I've constructed to head the Cairo gang. I remember meeting Charles Dance some years ago at the *Evening Standard* awards and ask Susie to send it to him. She doesn't think there's a chance in hell he'll accept it. We decide to send it to him anyway.

In the meantime we've opened offices in Dublin. The preproduction has started and already is in trouble. Having won the battle to shoot the whole film in Ireland, it is turning out to be more expensive than anybody thought. The success of the Section 35 tax breaks is such that everyone is working. So to crew up, we have to bring people in from England. This means hotel costs, per diems, air fares. And since Inland Revenue only admits the tax breaks to moneys spent in Ireland, wages paid to Irish nationals, that too is decreasing.

But the good news is that Tony Pratt has found a structure which he can use as a basis for the GPO set, and O'Connell Street. It is the rear of the Old Grange Gorman hospital, a listed building which is mostly in ruins. At least the set can be physically built now, which before seemed questionable.

Friday 7th April

Had a brainstorm at seven o'clock while running. Must be the wine from the night before. I call Steve Woolley at 7.45—still half asleep—and arrange to meet him and Red for breakfast.

Walk to Dart and meet them in the Davenport to talk about how we can control the extra people we're bringing in. Pat Clayton, my assistant director, wants to bring in three, Sandy Powell two, Red has alrady brought two, plus one extra accountant for Warners. The conversation gets nowhere and maybe there is no alternative.

I meet Alan Rickman and confirm him in the part of de Valera. He takes the news with equanimity, which is mildly disappointing. Or disconcerting. But he will be great. There is no alternative.

Rewrite the script in the afternoon. Take out the Mansion House scenes, which are history but dead wood. And under the influence of a period newspaper article, expand the Lincoln Jail escape. Introduce a tart's fur coat into the scene which might seem a bit burlesque, but is true, nonetheless.

Yvonne (my assistant) promptly loses the rewrites on her PC. Write them out again that night.

The guidelines for the Section 35 moneys are creating a reverse racism. Non-Irish crews almost have to wear a pink star. Makes for an unpleasant atmosphere.

One problem for me is the familiarity of the city and the history. What you live in you don't look at. What's part of you you don't make objective. Have to pretend I'm Russian or Japanese.

Monday 10th April

Charles Dance agrees to play Soames.

Rereading the script. It seems to move terribly fast. I have to get the passage of political events in there somehow—the ones that now are background. Success of Sinn Fein in the 1918 elections. The formation of the first Dail (parliament). The issues of the Treaty. If not dramatic as scenes in themselves, then as references within existing scenes. And Michael Collins has to propose to Kitty. At the moment it is assumed to have happened, but we don't see it. But the pace of the script would seem to demand more detail and authenticity of what the French call the *mise-en-scene*.

Shooting of the Cairo gang. Instead of a car roaring round the railing of Fitzwilliam Square, men running silently from the trees.

Collins to smoke cigarettes up to the arrival of the Black and Tans. Then to give them up.

Send script to Jim Sheridan.

Check boats of the period. Ferries to London.

The thing is to make the whole thing real, to take it out of the realm of hagiography and mythology, to make the period come alive as if it was today.

Things lacking in a story like this: a funeral and a hunger strike. Two things endemic to the mythology.

The election speech in Granard: make it clear that this was the first time an Irish electorate was being given a Republican choice.

Quote from Collins during the Treaty debates: 'You can have all the glory, let us have all the disgrace, but let us save Ireland.' (From Piaras Beaslai's biography.) A mixture of naivety and statesmanship.

As the production gets going, it becomes clear that what we need is an electronic library system. Every department builds up its own set of references—pictures, videos, newspaper cuttings, historical accounts etc. Mainly it builds them through ripping off the collections of the department in before them. Utter confusion, wherein no one knows for certain where anything is. If we could afford to make a CD-ROM of all the available information, aural print and visual, with space where each different department could add its own references and hand it to each Head of Department, it would make the whole procedure much saner. Would make computers more useful.

For example, there's the guerrilla leader Sean McEoins' description of Collins alighting from the train at Kingsbridge station from Ballinalee. As he walks towards the exit a Volunteer sidles past him whispers the address he is to head for.

And we have to get the structure of Collins's offices right. There were many of them, all over the city, each with its own 'cover' business. And there's the bike—always smeone to watch it. Or details like the hooded cloaks worn by West Cork women.

Friday 14th April. Good Friday

Down in Parknasilla with the family. Beautiful weather. Brenda, Daniel, Dashiell, my mother, Mary Coughaln and Frank, Anna and Georgia. On Wednesday met Michael Keating, the ex-Lord Mayor of Dublin and Kevin O'Conner, a journalist from the *Irish Independent*. They told me that an unnamed friend of Mr. Keating, a solicitor, is in possession of Emmet Dalton's diary. In the diary, the unnameable friend claims, there is an admission that Dalton shot Collins at close range with a Luger pistol. That Dev and Collins had arranged to meet but that radicals in both camps wanted to continue the fight so arranged for both of their executions. Dalton was to kill Collins; Liam Lynch, the head of the Irregulars, was to kill de Valera. Dalton got the opportunity and did it. So Collins died. Liam Lynch didn't, so de Valera survived.

The solicitor, who had been diagnosed as having terminal cancer, was in a state as to what to do with the papers. He had not released them previously because of the details he claimed they reveal about Collins's homosexual liaisons. Emmet Dalton's main job was to pick up young privates for Collins, apparently.

I ask them both have they seen the diaries. They say no, but they have photostats of certain pages—or printouts, I'm not sure. The whole scenario is far too fanciful, both neat and paranoid at the same time. I am not sure what they're approaching me for. I ask them and get an indeterminate reply. I tell them that if the diaries exist they should publish them. Then ask why they haven't insisted on viewing the documents themselves. They tell me, solemnly, that the cancer was misdiagnosed and the solicitor was no longer in fear of death, so no longer felt the burden of revealing his terrible secret. They leave and I'm left musing as to what an ex-TD (Trinity College, Dublin) and Lord Mayor and the political correspondent of a major Irish newspaper are doing peddling such extraordinary stories.

In the meantime, I have found someone to play Collins's killer. Jonathan Rees-Myers, from County Cork apparently, who looks like a young Tom Cruise. Comes into the casting session with alarming certainty. Obviously gifted.

Friday 21st April

Michael Collins, his namesake's nephew, walks into the office one afternoon and keeps me entertained with stories about his uncle for four hours. He brings the character alive. He must be in his eighties, but has more energy than me—is a cousin of Liam Collins, who is more retiring. I have to introduce him to Liam Neeson.

Thursday 27th April

Brad Pitt arrives in Dublin, comes out to dinner at the house. Brad is looking great and relaxed after the ordeal he was put through on *Interview*. He was quite unhappy on that film for all sorts of reasons and I hope I wasn't one of them.

Go out with him on the town some nights later. He has a minder with him and draws crowds wherever he goes. Sails through it all like one of Kerouac's dharma bums.

Tuesday 2 May

See Donal McCann at the Gate (Theatre) in Sebastian Barry's play *The Steward of Christendom*. Donal has gone on the dry, lost weight, and is generally as sharp as a razor. He gives an amazing performance and almost convinces me that the play is a great one. But I can't help wondering what it would be without him. Why is it that so many Irish plays now have the structure of a dream and use the language of poetry? There is a lack of astringency about the whole thing which is vaguely irritating. Characters drifting in and out of his consciousness as he lies on his sickbed. What is unique about it of course is that he plays a Royal Irish Constabulary man who laments the loss of the Empire. And the one figure he can relate to in the new régime that takes over is Michael Collins. This figure is becoming all things to everyone.

Monday 7th May

I watch *The Battle of Algiers* again. Odd, having met Gillo Pontecorvo in Venice. Gillo now so sedate, the film so ferocious. But what strikes me is that to show, as in that movie, the unstoppable movement of a people towards a concept like 'freedom' or 'nationhood' is to show a lie. Or to show, what we have come to realise in retrospect, is an untruth. Given the state of Algeria today, the complexity of the country Camus wrote about, the sense of moral certainty the film exudes seems naive and disingenuous. This is not to say that it is dishonest. But that its righteousness seems, from perspectives of twenty years, misplaced. The point being that political certainty excludes the tragic. When something as glittering as a future is posited, or a historical imperative, one either follows it and is right or ignores it and is wrong. No tragedy there. One goes with the perceived version of the future or ends up on Marx's dustbin of history. But the Irish situation can be seen as a particularly poignant, pitiless version of real tragedy. What was gained by the War of Independence would have come about anyway. Not soon enough perhaps, but it would have arrived. And it could be argued that the lasting effect of the war was partition, the Civil War and the 1937 constitution. The War of Independence was fought for rights that should have been granted decades ago, by the various aborted attempts at Home Rule. And what was gained in the end was a version of what parliamentary politics had long been promising, but had never delivered.

And the cost was partition, and the Civil War.

Therefore one can make a picture of it as if dissecting a recent corpse. Show the action and reaction. Show the choices the British Empire made that led to an irresistible drift towards violent solutions; the exhilaration of violence, the grotesque conclusions of its outcome. In other words, one examines human affairs as if they were at the mercy of an uncaring, corrosive destiny. A unique opportunity to tell a story born out of politics that allows for no political illusions. And the final definition of the actions of the hero as a tragic one. The contradictions of the politics drive him towards a tragic destiny.

Check around Grand Canal Street, and Boland's Mills, where de Valera held out against the British forces in 1916.

Thursday 11th May

I have to travel to New York for the Ireland America Award. The Irish American Foundation have set up a marquee in Central Park where one of these large charity dinners is held. Tony O'Reilly hosts it, all sorts of Irish-American billionaires there. This is the other side of the coin to Noraid I suppose. They go to opera rather than movies, breed horses, know the country through its stud farms. I sit with Mr. O'Reilly and his charming wife throughout the dinner and can't bring myself to mention the fact that I am suing his newspaper, the *Sunday Independent* for libel.

Sunday 14th May

Use Julia for herself, what she is and what she does naturally. Make sure the accent is untraceable.

The scenes around Bloody Sunday: a disturbing tinge of the erotic between them. Make the connection with the violence outside explicit. A vase of roses in the hotel room with which he strokes her face. Red roses.

Check small alleyways off Thomas Street. (Sounds like I'm plotting an assassination.)

Treat them as fictional characters. Treat history as fiction in the making: a fiction that will create the future.

Wednesday 31st May

Bloody Sunday. Get an accurate account of the massacres of the Cairo gang.

Gleeson's account of the Croke Park killings much more gruesome than the script. Tans advancing in a line, then firing.

Aidan Quinn's research on Harry Boland—the nightmare of every actor seeing the film from their character's point of view.

If Liam can show the dark humour beneath the Collins character it would make it spectacular. As in Tim Pat Coogan's quote—'he knew well the dark, loving forces that surrounded him'.

Change names of Ned Broy and Vinnie Byrne? But would that solve anything?

Rewrite the Dail debates to demonstrate what the argument and division was about. Essential to show the conviction and veracity of the Republican perspective.

Saturday 3rd June

Use some of the real descriptions of Bloody Sunday. Intercut from shape of Kitty lying on the bed to shape of wife or whore beside officer.

Flowers delivered by maid. Flowers handled by Kitty. Detail to detail, intimacy to intimacy.

1916. Shocking in the casual way they are dispatched. Matched by Collins's actions of Bloody Sunday.

Watched Bertolucci's *The Conformist*. The corrosion of a soul of an ordinary, conforming human being, conforming to Fascism but stumbling too far. Why am I watching these movies again? What surprised me was the beauty and depth of it. The sensuality of the train journey, with the wife he knew he did not love.

What Collins is best at is appalling. And in some way he appalls himself. A divided heart. But a magnificent one. He refuses to hide. And they all, gradually, from a starting point of innocence, become involved in a game of blood and betrayal that can only have one outcome. Historical necessity as a malignant god.

Trying to imagine a scene with Kitty. Where he kisses her, by the station.

The Four-Alls. Some dancing happening in the village square outside the pub. People running towards it. In the pub, he performs to draw attention to himself. So his killers will be drawn towards him. So he can talk to them . . .

Monday 5th June

Chris Menges and Mike Roberts arrive in Dublin. Mike the best operator there is, who drinks three pints of Guinness at lunchtime and ten at night, chainsmokes and always gets it in the first take. He is working with Chris for the first time since *The Mission*. They make a wonderful team yet you would hardly know it to be around them, like a husband and wife who know each other too well. So with Pat Clayton (first assistant director), Yves De Bono (special effects supervisor), Steve Woolley, Redmond Morris and twenty or so others, we begin the trudge round locations in a series of minibuses. The number of locations is so vast that it takes us six solid days, fourteen hours a day, to see them all.

I can see the look of growing horror on their faces as

the realisation sinks in that the film is a logistical night-mare, an organisational impossibility. The amount of extras we're hoping to fill the streets with, the period vehicles and weapons, the days on which we're hoping for an open pub-lic call, to recruit the thousands we can't afford, not to mention the location moves that are scheduled every day. But the sheer ambition of the thing has its own sense of liberation. Instead of asking why, I suppose you ask why not. And it is the worst stage in a movie, where you see the whole thing at once, you see all the problems of a fourteen-week schedule over a series of days. But I have a theory. The hectic pace that the schedule demands of us will set up its own energy, keep everything fresh, and that energy will be most evident in the acting. We'll have to shoot most of the film in developing master shots, encompassing entire scenes, with very little cover, with multiple cameras for the large action scenes; and the cast we have chosen will re-spond beautifully to that. The worst thing that can happen on a film is for the performances to get bogged down—in questions of meaning, characterisation, worries about dia-logue. On this, they won't have a chance.

One still unsolved mystery of the whole enterprise is Collins's death. Not who shot him, but where we will shoot him. We can't afford to go to Beal na mBlath, which would probably be unsuitable anyway, and can't find a road with the over hanging bluffs that would be appropriate for the ambush. But wandering round the environs of Hollywood Country Wicklow, a small town where we will shoot the Four-Alls pub sequences, I find a tiny glacial valley. It is hidden by a small hill from the main road, but the minute I climb it, I can see that it's perfect. As if a chisel had gouged into a mountainside, a meandering gulf sur-rounded by steep hills on either side, there is something genuinely magical about it. The only problem being that there is no road. Where the road should be is a swamp. I propose to the production that we build the road we need and the reaction is predictable. The director's gone nuts again.

But I climb with Chris Menges to the top of this little wonderland and know that it's right. Chris remembers shooting a documentary with Tibetan rebels, during the course of which they ambushed a Chinese army convoy. The parameters of that Tibetan valley were just the same. So it must be right. Terry Apse, the construction manager, takes a look at it and surmises that with a series of earth-movers and gravel-trucks it could be done. And bit by bit the unimaginable seems to enter the realms of possibility.

Monday 12th June

After recce, discuss with Liam scene of Boland's return. We have found a dock in Alexandra Basin where they can play the lines over the water. If the lines will play that way.

Thursday 15th June

Rewrites. Cut exterior Harcourt Street. Cut burning of Limerick. Substitute slow hanging, a favourite torture method at the time. It takes a long time to hang a man. Place schoolroom in abattoir.

Warners worried about the bleakness of the ending. I come up with a scene I'm not entirely convinced of. After the ambush a kid comes down the road, leading a herd of goats. See the bullet casings. Begin to fill his pockets with them. Then finds Michael Collins' cap. Places it on his tiny head. Walks down the valley whistling. I'm sure this will change again, since endings are always the most difficult for me.

Tuesday 20th June

Begin rehearsals. I have never really rehearsed on a film before—just done read-throughs, where we discussed the character and any problems with the dialogue. I suppose I've used them as a means to rewrite if the actors find some aspects of the character a bad fit. But on this I know I have to take rehearsals seriously. We will be moving so fast, have such a large cast of characters, some of the actors may never meet again outside the confines of this room, so it's essential everyone knows where they're going. So we sit down, everyone makes their introductions and we begin to read. And some way into the reading, I realise an extraordinary thing is taking place. My fears about the historical nature of the characters prove utterly groundless. Everyone has researched their part, even down to the smallest player. Where they came from, their accents, their habits, whether they smoked or not (most of them did). And I can see we're not trying to revive Caesar or Napoleon here, but we're dealing with characters to whom these actors have direct access. Through reading, through folk memory, through conversations with their descendants. And even through the continuing moral and political arguments which the characters' actions gave rise to. As a director I've just got to sit back and watch it happen. And I realise once more that it's not the performance that is important. It's the reality behind the performance. In this case, that reality is palpable.

I was surprised and a little alarmed by how much historical information there was in the dialogue. It seemed to move through speeches. Have to keep an eye on this.

For Liam—get him to use the accent as a sardonic, psychological toy. Sure why wouldn't I, boy? The way Cork people bring out the accent when they want to express irony. Or conceal something.

Croke Park—a top shot, seeing the armoured vehicle will not work. We have to see the crowds behind the thing as it shoots. Track around it to show both ends of the stadium.

The amount of violence in Bloody Sunday. Find a way to make it gripping, not nauseating.

Write additional material for dancing scene before the truce. A racing metaphor.

There is no way of knowing how far the audience's sympathies will go with our characters, given the nature of what they do.

Sunday 2nd July

We begin shooting on a Sunday, since we have to close off the whole of Dames Street down to Trinity College. Start with the biggest set-up, the families of British officers running for the safety of Dublin Castle after they've got the news of the Bloody Sunday assassinations. Every set-up is large but exhilarating. Pat Clayton marshals the crowds like a British officer himself, with tremendous efficiency. He's broken them down by class, age, sex. The whole of Dames Street has been transformed, a statue of Queen Victoria straddling its centre.

Charles Dance drops by and says, 'you like to jump in at the deep end, don't you?'

The main problem is to keep the crowds of onlookers away. Everywhere I turn the camera they're staring. Get through five scenes—and the one that is compromised may be the most important. The shooting of Smith, the Dublin detective, is left till the end and it proves impossible to cover it in the time left. The kid chosen to pull the dray horses and bring Smith's car to a halt so he can be shot doesn't function. His face is impenetrable and he doesn't take instruction. I'll have to pick up some close shots on it later. But the fact that we've got through it all makes it seem the schedule might be possible.

Monday 3rd July

A strangely affecting morning. We shoot the handover of Dublin Castle to the Free State army by the British forces. The Last Post played as the Union Jack comes down. Mary Robinson, the current President of Ireland drives through in mid-shot to attend a meeting of the Forum For Peace And Reconciliation. Liam salutes her, in uniform. I don't know if she returns the gesture.

Anyway, the flag comes down, something David Leanish about the whole procedure. British crew are oddly affected, as am I. I ask Stephen Woolley why this is so. He says probably because they left under duress and left a mess.

And after that bout of nostalgia we get down to serious business of blowing things up. Charles Dance and his SS men arrive, drive through a courtyard full of Black and Tans hung with more gun-belts than Pancho Villa's men.

Another scene with Ian McIlhenny, playing Redmond the detective, arriving with reinforcements from Belfast, storming into his car which immediately explodes.

The level of co-operation we are getting from the authorities is really remarkable. The President of the country in session with the Forum in the morning, us blowing cars sky-high in the afternoon. I can only hope the ironies remain fictional.

Saturday 8th July

A break after the first week. We're moving at a ferocious pace, one or two takes for the large set-ups, most of the acting scenes done in single developing shots. The actors seem to love it and it's releasing a storm of energy in Liam in particular. And not only the actors, the entire crew, down to the extras seem to know what to do. Directing them is mostly a matter, on my part, of staying out of the way. In fact the strongest impression I have is of a story waiting to burst. Maybe because it has remained unmade for so long. Or maybe because this particular part of Irish history was an embarrassed secret for so long, told in metaphors, never told straight. And when I think of it, O'Casey was the first and the best revisionist. His version of these events was told from a snug in an O'Connell Street bar. One can't debunk historical pieties more effectively than that.

In the day exteriors we have to accept whatever natural light there is, which can make cameramen unhappy, but Chris compensates by keeping his hand on the remote iris. The days are too bright and in their period suits the actors are in danger of seeming to be in 1920s Chicago.

The boldness of the silhouettes. It's becoming like a signature for the film. Keep it that way.

Cast: Make sure all the smaller parts are consistent with the principals.

Brendan Gleeson (Liam Tobin): Include him in the Beal na mBlath scenes. Have him play the fiddle in the Four-Alls pub, since he's so good at it.

Monday 10th July

Scene 60, where Collins tells O'Reilly, Cullen and Harry Boland that he is going to start a war. Liam (Neeson) lying by a writing desk, exhausted after a night going through the Castle files. Others come in successively, asking where the hell has he been. We've conceived it in rehearsal as a monologue, delivered out of his half-sleep, his mind ticking in overdrive, the end of which is a letter delivered to the Castle detectives. If they don't leave, they'll be shot. Chilling moment where Aidan realises they will have to do it. Could you bear it? The performances go from banter and mutual abuse to utter seriousness. Can't be bad.

Sunday 16th July

Four days with Stephen Rea. The scenes with Stephen and Liam are a bit like having Humphrey Bogart and Robert Mitchum in the same film together. Today we end up on a bridge near Laytown over the Nanny River. For some reason if I'm stuck for a location in a film, we always end up here. I used it in *Angel,* in *The Crying Game* and now in this. Spent a lot of my childhood on the strand below. My father died after a day's fishing on the river beneath. I don't choose it for sentimental reasons, it just seems to suit a certain kind of emotion. One of impending doom, I suppose.

While we are setting up a wide shot, both the actors are standing on the bridge with umbrellas, as it is raining. The umbrellas add a marvellous delicacy to it, like a Japanese woodcut, the black outlined against the sea behind, the fragility overwhelmed by the mass of the railway tracks above. I try to persuade them to do the scene with umbrellas. They resist, and I don't know why. Maybe the umbrellas seem effeminate. Maybe their heads can't get close enough. Half-way through the arguments, the rain stops, so I lose. But I'll always regret the loss of those umbrellas.

Wednesday 19th July

Two scenes with Aidan and Liam, at either end of the picture, at either end of the rupture of their relationship. Chris has persuaded me to shoot the latter one, a night scene, lit by moonlight coming through the windows, which are flowing with rain. So one gets the effect of moving water over their faces. I remember the scene in *Rebecca,* a daylight one, which used a similar effect. Bright sunlight coming through the windows, reflecting rivulets of rain over the actors' faces. The problem is, when it rains the sun doesn't shine. Nor does the moon, if it ever shines anyway. But the effect has its own poetry. The other problem is, the actors must be persuaded they would not turn on the lights. We get through the lack of logic, though, and I see he is right. The atmosphere of the darkened room, the only light an aqueous one from the windows, the sound of dripping water is sad and perfect.

Tuesday 25th July

The first of our large open crowd-calls in Rathdrum, Co. Wicklow, which is doubling as Granard. We have sunk all the telephone lines, repainted every exterior in the town. Liam has to deliver a speech I've written for Collins, for the 1918 elections. The police will charge, the crowd will rebuff them and he'll be dragged into the yard of the Granard Arms where he'll meet Kitty Kiernan for the first time. So we set up the cameras and wait for the crowds to drift in.

Eventually they come, more than two thousand of them, but the trouble is I recognise more than a few Dublin journalists hiding under period caps. Liam delivers his speech magnificently with all the gestures of Collins we saw in the newsreels, then the police charge and a bare-knuckle fist-fight breaks out. I can see quite a few old scores are being settled between those from the different townlands, some real blood is split. We have stuntmen there to protect the actors but they can't stop Aidan from smashing his hurley off the back of a beefy extra who managed to get a dig through. One can only do this kind of thing so many times before someone gets seriously hurt.

Wednesday 26th July

Same locations, same crowds. Now a speech from Liam in the aftermath of the Treaty débâcle. More controlled chaos this time, with a platform in flames, gunfire erupting from among the crowds, a bunch of horses driven through to disrupt them. Julia makes her first entrance, pushing through the mayhem to put a gun to the head of machine-gun-toting anti-Treatyite.

The press are everywhere, generally in ridiculous disguises. We drag photographers from under Julia's trailer, from the rooftops, but it's impossible to keep them away.

She does her first real scene thankfully inside, sings 'She Moved Through the Fair' just the way my sister did.

Sunday 30th July

Shoot the scene at Kingsbridge Station where Collins and Kitty see Harry to the station, on his way to America. 'There's a butterfly been seen in West Clare . . .' I have always wanted to photograph a woman in a period hat saying goodbye to her lover as the train draws him away. Maybe it seemed the epitome of romanticism to me. Anyway, I finally get to do it. Mike manages to adjust the camera as the train draws off, to hold Aidan, retreating in the background, framed by her hat, before she turns.

Thursday 3rd August

Over the week a whole spate of articles has appeared—'I Was An Extra with Michael Collins'. There's no way of stopping them, so one just has to ride with it.

Julia Roberts is taking on the part with a simplicity that makes the eye of the camera melt. Trouble is, she cannot dye her hair—because she needs it like that for her next part—so she's wearing a wig which tends to fan out behind her head like a bunch of leaves. So I'm constantly on hair watch. I met her first when she and Liam were an item, on the set of *High Spirits*. One is always worried when actors have had a prior relationship, but here the worries are unfounded. The scenes on the night of bloody Sunday are done without any groping, thank God. That was her instinct and she was right. I manage to place a rose between their faces. Can orchestrate them into almost romanesque compositions. They cry when he says: 'Promise me you'll never care about me.' I'm always wary of tears, but these seem to flow naturally, like water.

An article by Kevin Myers during the week in the English *Daily Telegraph* claims Collins was a bloody-minded psychopath. (I wonder what that makes Winston Churchill?) A 'complex one' whose War of Independence achieved nothing. Quotes me on 'the appalling nature of the savagery and the necessity of it at the same time'. What I meant was the inevitability of it.

If one were to argue the historical point one would have to mention so many things. The secession of Ulster from the Home Rule Act before 1916. The fact that the capitulation of the British Government to the Ulster Volunteers made a physical force movement in the South inevitable. And the total collapse of the Irish Parliamentary party in the 1918 elections, with its replacement by the broad Sinn Fein movement. It represented the collapse of British Parliamentary politics in Ireland under huge popular pressure; and the entry of a wholly new element into Irish politics. The *ennui* and desire for a more dignified exit from a relationship with the Empire should be put in context. And the context surely has to be the ferocious resistance of the Empire to any attempt to fracture its parts. Ireland was the first. The North of Ireland may be the last.

The main opposition to this film will be from within this country. There's a series of resentments, sectarian and class differentiations that disguise themselves here as politics.

And maybe the main objection is that the story is being told at all, in any form. The old form of censorship was simpler. At least it allowed one the simplicity of exile. Anyway, the release and all the fuss it causes might be fun.

On a more comfortingly routine note, the art department costs are running wildly over. And I can see why. The logistical scale of the picture is huge. Merely dressing the locations costs a fortune. The less they find here, the more they have to bring in, and the one thing they can't do is leave the next day's location unprepared. The only way to save money is to get ahead of schedule. But to do that we'd have to spend even more.

Friday 4th August

A series of scenes in Clery's shop, where Kitty buys a wedding dress, to be intercut with Michael's death.

The minute Julia put on the dress, a pall of gloom falls over her. I don't know what it is, don't want to ask. I think she has a problem doing emotionally depressing scenes. It's understandable, but the way it affects her is unsettling.

We spend all day inside, then walk down to Dun Laoire Pier for a shot we have planned months ago. A full-page scene, done in one shot, at the magic hour. We have cleared the harbour of boats and substituted our own period ones. What we cannot stop, though, is the Sealink Ferry to Holyhead. So we have a window of forty minutes, when the light will be right and the ferry absent. We begin to rehearse, and Julia's spirits seem to have lifted. Two men and a woman walking arm-in-arm, talking about a horse race that has been won, and trying to estimate the odds on the success or failure of their own small battle. We get several perfect takes, though her accent slips towards the end. And that will have to be fixed later since the light is gone.

Tuesday 8th August

The Macushla Scene. Or should I say the scene where Michael Collins, Harry Boland and Kitty Kiernan hear the news of the Truce. But Frank Paterson will sing 'Macushla' with the Café Orchestra, which we have changed into a waltz from McCormack's beautiful ballad. The three-four tempo seems to help it, actually. The song itself has such overwhelming melancholy that it needs some uplift.

Chris has lit the tea-room in the Mansion House with a cornucupia of bare bulbs hanging from the ceiling. He made the point that electricity was new to the world and people over-indulged in it, like a Coney Island at the time. Anyway, the effect is brilliant.

How does one convey happiness, exaltation? Those scenes in American movies where characters are hugging each other in delight I always find embarrassing. We have one of them here, but decide to draw the camera away from it at their moment of maximum relief and happiness. The camera rises up on a crane to reveal the light bulbs, framing them from above. It darkens the issue somehow, which is appropriate, since the outcome won't be happy. It also seems like a concluding shot in a film, but our story is only halfway through. I hope it recovers.

Wednesday 9th August

One of the biggest of our crowd days, and our first on the large O'Connell Street set. We need cheering crowds to celebrate the news of the Truce, cheering crowds to celebrate de Valera's escape from the Lincoln Jail, and an almighty, murderous crowd to receive his famous 'rivers of blood' speech.

We had hoped for five thousand, but by midday have heard that there are twice that number trying to get in. How many make it on to the set I don't know, but the crush is alarming, almost uncontrollable. For the Truce celebrations I attempt to get them at random, the way crowds are. But the chaos becomes almost unmanageable, the thousands at the back trying to crush forward to see what is going on, making it dangerous round the camera.

We shoot what we can of that, then move them up towards the GPO, where we have built a platform for de Valera's speech. This famous and much-criticised speech was made just before the Civil War and is held by many as the main instigation of the outbreak of hostilities. Alan Rickman will speak de Valera's actual words. It is his first scene in the movie. He, an English actor, has to play an Irish icon in front of six thousand people from all over the country. It's only when I bring him up on the platform that I realise what I've done. Alan is as tense as an actor can be, which I tell myself must be appropriate. Anyway, I begin haranguing the crowds, telling them how they should react, and they get into the swing of it. Then Alan takes over. The transformation is extraordinary. His voice comes with a furious high-pitched passion; his movements, like a jerky marionette, and the mathematical, archaic precision of his diction—all bear an uncanny resemblance to the man himself. And after the speech the crowd says nothing. I had asked them to react, take sides, but I think they are stunned into silence. I get on the bullhorn again and tell them about the passions this speech would give rise to. Then Alan goes to it once more. His words are drowned by roars of argument, roars of approval, all contradicting one another.

After shooting, I go to his trailer to tell him how great he was. He glares at me balefully and says: You wouldn't do that to an American actor.

Wednesday 16th August

We begin the serious mayhem. Have to shoot the 1916 sequence of the GPO being blasted to bits by the British forces. In actual fact O'Connell Street was razed by a gunship from the River Liffey, but we would have to rebuild the whole city to do that. As it is, we have imported artillery from England which comes with a terrifyingly efficient gun-crew. The officer in charge, a small man with an alarmingly precise moustache and military manner, is so good that I cast him as, well, the officer in charge. We have six cameras and rehearse in sequence the explosions that will wreck the building, the foreground and background action. The sun is hot, which is bad, but we can't afford to wait for cloud. When any further delays seem pointless, I decide to go for it, call action and all hell breaks loose.

Operating a camera in circumstances like these must be a bit like being a gunner in an actual battle situation. The noise is deafening, the smoke casts a pall of confusion over everything. Sitting behind a bank of monitors, I can see some of the camera operators responding to their ears rather than their eyes. A bang is heard and a camera pans, trying to find the source of it. The confusion is, I suppose, understandable, and sometimes even a badly framed shot adds to the documentary reality of it all. After the smoke dies down, we rest and do it all again. There is a reality to the scene that is quite inescapable and I thank heaven that we have decided not to use any optical enhancement, as is the norm these days. There is all the difference in the world between an optical process and the real thing.

The next day we film the actual surrender. A crane-shot, cleaving down the pillars of the building to find Michael Collins, Harry Boland, Pearse, MacDonagh, Tom Clarke, Countess Markiewicz, all the leaders of the 1916 Rising, emerging from the ruined building. They are marched down toward the Rotunda, in full view of a bemused popu- lace. It is too sad for words. John Boorman has come down for the day with one of the first motion-picture cameras the Lumière brothers used, to shoot his part of a French series on the centenary of cinema. Multiple ironies here, I sup- pose. A camera of the period shooting a contemporary cam- era and crew shooting a film of the period. I look through the eyepiece of the hundred-year-old box at the scene and wonder should I have shot the film in black and white. But only for a moment.

Tuesday 22nd August

We shoot the executions of the 1916 signatories in Kilmain- ham Jail. The square at the time was ringed by tiny cabins, where the prisoners would break stones like an American chain-gang. But the bareness of it as it is without them seems more appropriate. Pearse is the first to be shot. I try to frame it like the Goya painting, *The Third of May 1808,* but can't get the camera quite far enough back. Pearse dies well but the extra attempting to play the Franciscan monk who read the last rites makes a haims of the blessing, so we send down to Adam and Eve's for a real monk. Tom Clarke is next. Clarke is played by Ger O'Leary, who is normally cast in Dublin theatre as James Larkin. Ger plays it with extraordinary dignity. Once again, I suppose, a case of the history informing the actor, and once again all I have to do is let it happen. Then comes Connolly, carried into the execution square on a stretcher, tied to a chair. I place the camera behind him for the shooting, so the bullets throw the blood and pieces of wood from the chair back towards the lens. Chris Menges thinks I'm being ghoulish, but given the norm in contemporary cinema, I think it is mild.

Then inside the prison, for the scene where de Valera writes the letter to Collins that will put the executions in context and outline their tactics for the future. It is Alan Rickman's idea to speak as he writes. I had written his words as a voiceover, but his choice turns out to be quite brilliant. He somehow becomes a father to the Republic and a father to Collins. A father who will betray him.

Monday 28th August

Harry Boland was shot in a small hotel in Skerries, by the sea. A hotel by the sea of the period was impossible to find, however so for months I racked my brains trying to think of an alternative. Then the location manager brought me to an abandoned bondage warehouse down by the docks—a listed building called Stack A. The building was a multiple problem-solver—serving as locations for the secret Dail meetings, a meeting point for the Squad after various jobs, and most important, a location for the death of Harry Boland. I decided to call the location the Catacombs, a name suggested by the maze of underground tunnels beneath the building. So we're here now shooting Harry Boland's last moments. Chris has had holes drilled at various points in the vaulted ceilings, so light can spill downwards from the floors above. We have worked out the shots in advance, the lighting in advance, and the sequence works like clockwork, which just goes to show that most of the creativity in a movie takes place in the preparation. If you haven't prepared, no amount of genius can save a sequence from the cutting-room floor.

The place is quite dangerous, however. While scouting it, Chris Menges suddenly vanished and I had to jump into a hole in the ground, where there seemed to be some kind of underground river to pull him out. So Aiden Quinn is now running full-tilt through these tunnels, on the wet slabbed floors, Mike Roberts on a motorbike in front of him with a hand-held camera. If he slipped, I hate to think of the consequences. But Aidan is not one to run at half-speed, and thankfully he doesn't.

Tuesday 29th August

Harry Boland has made his escape and is floundering across the Liffey. By the grounds of Stack A there is an old dry-dock, now full of filthy Liffey water. Aidan is in a wet-suit, swimming towards what he thinks is his freedom when a Free State trooper on the banks above throws a cigarette in the water. He turns, sees his doom and Yves De Bono shoots pellets in the water and activates the blood bag in his neck. One camera on a raft, two more on the banks above. The blood spurts, makes a mess in the water and we pull him out. It has to work, because I don't think I can get him in the water twice.

What I haven't worked out is how Michael Collins comes upon the scene and finds Boland's body. But thankfully there is an old industrial crane by the dry-dock. We manage to make it function and hang Aidan from the chain so his body is being winched and swung from the water to the roadside as Collins arrives.

'What happened? Who closed your eyes?' are the lines I'd written as Michael Collins touches the face of his dead companion. I'm always nervous of my own tendency towards poeticised diction, maybe it's a curse of the Irish. But Liam gives the lines the reality they need. And for once I can make Aidan's profile loom over his, since he's suspended four feet above the ground.

Thursday 31st August

Billed as a night and dawn shoot. It becomes a night and day shoot. We begin with the arrest of Cathal Brugha, in the beginning of the story. We continue with the scene on the Liffey dry-dock, down near the Alexandra basin, where Michael Collins awaits Harry Boland's return from America. Having finally tracked down a period motor-launch we are ready to shoot this pivotal scene. The background to it—or the subtext, as some would have it—is that Boland returns from something like a promotional tour or holiday, to greet Collins, who back home has gone through literal hell. The rigours of the Black and Tan war,

Bloody Sunday, the massacres at Croke Park. 'You look like a gangster,' Mick shouts across the water. 'And you look like a ghost,' Harry shouts back. And the scene has an appropriately eerie quality, the mist shining on the water, the dark figure of Liam in the foreground as the glistening boat drifts towards him.

Somehow Liam manages to convey both exhaustion and infinite resilience at the same time. He knows how little he needs to do. But the problem is that the location we've chosen affords only one angle. Turn the camera round for reverses and something like a car graveyard is revealed behind him. We struggle with this problem for most of the evening and basically lose the battle. We also lose the dawn, since the light creeps up on us.

By the time we get to Sandymount Strand for the third location, it is clear daylight. A sequence we had planned for magic hour, where Mick and Harry cycle from de Valera's house back to Dublin across the mudflats, has turned into a day scene. Everyone is so exhausted it seems ludicrous to go on, but the exhaustion is such that no one has the energy to call a halt. So we start shooting, with a stedicam on the back of a car. The sound will be useless, the vehicles gouge tracks in the sand, for each new take we have to push the action further out towards sea, I'm manning the video playback and forget to push the buttons each time. A situation where the crew should probably assassinate the director. But maybe exhaustion prevents them.

Monday 4th September

Shooting one of the Boody Sunday killings. The squad surround an officer who is exercising in Fitzwilliam Square at first light. Malcolm Douglas, an actor who was in the first television play I wrote, plays the officer. Brendan Gleeson told me how they would ask their victims did they want to say a prayer, and before the prayer had concluded would pull the trigger. One of the most bizarre concepts of mercy I've ever come across. We devise a track round the officer's face, a series of handguns pointed to his head as he prays. Then the camera tracks past the officer, isolates Brendan's face and he pulls the trigger. For the first time I wonder about the moral perspectives of what we're doing. The scene is so brutal and pitiless. The prayer gives the officer an inescapable dignity. Then I realise it has to be that way. The only way to make it less disturbing would be to cast the officer in a villainous light, the ultimate dishonesty. It must have been that brutal. And the presentation of it should make an audience question their moral parameters.

Tuesday 5th September

We blow up O'Connell Street again, this time for the Civil War. The Free State forces finish what the British began. And this time the warfare is much more messy. Small arms fire up and down the street, half-trained guerrillas being blown out of buildings, returning fire with improvised mortars. And the shoddily clad Free State army improvising with British artillery and armoured gun-cars. We are trying to give the impression of the arbitrary nature of this kind of conflict and keep that camera moving all the time, huge explosions often seen out of the edge of frame. I have the feeling that the sequence has somehow to centre round the face of Harry Boland and so we improvise a shot of Aidan inside a draper's shop, edging behind a pillar as the bombs fall outside, shattering the plate-glass windows between him and the street. We shoot it at thirty-six frames, Aidan firing at an unseen assailant, then dropping the gun, wondering what has he done.

Thursday 7th September

A series of scenes in the Mansion House. De Valera informs Michael Collins he will be part of the team that negotiates the Treaty with England. Collins rails against going, but to no avail. Then, the crucial scene where de Valera confronts Collins about the Treaty he eventually signed.

The first centres round a track on Collins's face, aghast at what has been proposed. Camera tracks down a long table, to reveal the cabinet, staring at him. Ends with de Valera in the foreground. This is the point at which the story will change, the most worrying one in the script, where the argument with Britain fades and the argument amongst themselves begins. Liam is all directness, straight confrontation. Alan is as intricate as an spider's web. We discuss how Churchill described negotiation with de Valera as 'trying to pick up mercury with a fork'. To which Dev replied, 'Why doesn't he try a spoon?'

I suppose the question behind the scene is why de Valera didn't go himself, with his superb strategic and political skills. And the parallel with the current negotiations between Sinn Fein and the British government is inescapable. The obvious tactic would have been to keep Collins, as the militarist, behind and for Dev to exercise his talents in London. My conclusion in the screenplay is that de Valera didn't go because, in the course of his prior negotiations to see whether there was any basis for talks, he learned that they were not willing to go far enough. He sent Collins, first in the hope that he could get a better deal and, secondly, because he didn't want to be associated with any compromise that might result.

The real puzzle, though, is why the eventual argument over the Treaty centered on the Oath of Allegiance and not the partition of the country. The disturbing thought is that all parties concerned had implicitly accepted partition as a fact long before the Treaty; had accepted, after the formation of the Ulster Volunteers and the Government of Ireland Act 1920, that some separate accommodation would have to be made there. This is one issue my script doesn't deal with at all. I would love to if it were possible, but given that the argument between Dev, Boland and Collins was about the Oath, not about the North, it is difficult to introduce it. As it was, Collins seems to have been alone among politicians on both sides of the argument in his concern for the Northern minority, sending men and arms up there, even when it made a mockery of the Treaty he had signed.

This will all become an issue when we film the Treaty debates next week. As it is, we've got to photograph de Valera's confrontation with Collins after his return home. The contemporary accounts describe de Valera as being in a 'towering rage', and Alan Rickman flies around the Mansion House room hurling spittle and a copy of the Treaty itself at a submissive Liam. There is a point at which the antagonisms in the story have to change. From a confrontation between the British and the Irish, the film has to shift gear into a far more tragic confrontation between Collins and de Valera. As we shoot the scene, and Alan concludes it in salamander-like silence, I sense we've arrived at this point. But I'll only know when I cut it together.

Sunday 10th September

The scenes scheduled are at the Four Courts, where Collins fires at the occupied building across the river with British guns, thus beginning the Civil War in earnest. We have a morning in which to stage the bombardment. Amazingly, the powers-that-be have allowed us to place controlled explosions all over the historic façade. The shooting falls into two halves. The first, where we cover the bombardment, and the resultant carnage, with multiple camera. The second, a long tracking shot where Collins walks away in disgust at what he has done while bombardment continues behind him.

The usual chaos results. The effects are perfectly prepared, the stuntmen fly through the air, return fire as planned, but the noise, smoke and confusion seem to outwit several of the cameras. So we set it up again, trying to cover what we missed. By which time it's almost lunch and everyone's running round like headless chickens wondering should we break or not.

Yves De Bono, the effects supervisor, says he can prepare enough explosions for one take before we break and I decide to do that. We lay the track, rehearse it with Liam and Mike Roberts, the first camera operator, by which time a large crowd of Dubliners has gathered behind us. By now Yves's explosives are primed so I call action and the building rocks once more, now to much more spectacular effect. Liam strides off down by the Liffey wall in disgust, Ian Hart (Joe O'Reilly) running at his heels, as the Four Courts mushrooms behind him with clouds of smoke and dust. The take is perfect and the crowds behind the camera erupt into spontaneous applause. Just as I call cut, the skies open. An equatorial torrent of rain flood down on us, turning the streets into a river. An extraordinary piece of luck, since if we'd waited half an hour, the explosive charges and the whole day would have been washed out.

In the late afternoon we have another stroke of luck. We have spent months wondering how we would get the River Liffey into the picture, a wide perspective on it, with the city behind, since the river is the city, in the Joycean sense. The scene is one where the first news of the popular vote in favour of the Treaty comes out, a quite conventional shot, beginning on a paperseller calling out the morning's news, then jibbing up to reveal an expanse of river with the Four Courts beyond. Mike Roberts changes the lens to the widest one we have and asks me to have a look. The result is fabulous—the river seen curving to almost infinity, the city behind it from the Four Courts right up to the Wellington monument of the Phoenix Park. Because the sun is low and the scene is backlit, the light has lost its defining power and none of the modern buildings show through. The only problem is we have to stop all modern traffic for a distance of up to six miles. Somehow Pat Clayton gets his assistants to do that, clogging up the entire north side of Dublin, but delivering to the film a shot that I thought could only be done by spending half a million dollars on a model and computer-generated effects.

Tuesday 12th September

De Valera's escape from Lincoln Jail. The contemporary accounts of this event read almost like a farce. De Valera, while serving Mass in the jail, noticed a set of keys swinging from the priest's surplice. He managed to get his hands on them and sent an imprint to Collins in Dublin. The jail, apparently, was trawled by hookers so they dressed de Valera in a fur coat and feathered hat and pretended to be two punters as they whisked him away. It is one of the few moments in the story where the three of them can express humour together, so I've written it as farcically as the history suggests.

The exterior of Kilmainham Jail is doubling as Lincoln. We surround it with mist and with what Pat Clayton (first assistant director) quaintly calls ladies of the night. If the camera were to shift a millimetre to the left or the right it would reveal where we are, but the scene seems to be working. Alan Rickman looks like an angular spinster in the fur coat. Those of us who know the legend of de Valera and his rigid Catholicism find the scene amusing and I can only hope that those who don't will find it equally so. And it has to be said that anyone as conscious of the dignity of his persona as de Valera was must have had some sense of the absurd.

Sunday 17th September

The invention of the motion picture and of the internal combustion engine happened around the same time. And the one was determined to outwit the other. In the thirties and forties they had one solution to shooting inside cars. A projected image of the retreating streets and the actors inside the car on a soundstage. Now, in the interests of realism, we have to drag the car through real streets on tracking vehicles of various kinds while the director sits up front with headphones and a video monitor and screams action above the screeching engines, and the actors mouth their lines inside. If the actor is driving, he swings the useless steering wheel to the left and the right, always two beats later than the vehicle itself. The absurd unreality of it all makes real acting impossible, one does take after take at random until the magazine is empty and just hopes one has covered the scene. Today we have a scene where Michael Collins walks off the Liverpool Ferry, pushes his way through crowds of reporters to a car where Harry Boland is waiting for him. Then follows a conversation inside the car, two pages of dialogue in which Mick tries to justify to his friend the deal he has struck.

There are two problems. The first, how to act with any sense of emotional commitment when the circumstances are so alienating. The second, that even if we wanted to shoot it with a tracking vehicle, there are no period streets long enough available in Dublin to provide an acceptable background. The solution, when we come to it, is admirably simple. We lay all the track we have—more than two hundred feet—alongside the boat, create a jam of dockside traffic through which the car must make its way as they have their conversation. So Liam can walk down the ramp, push his way through the crush, take his seat beside Aidan, and the car can drive off with the camera tracking alongside. The actors can act, I can hear them, discuss each take with them and the scene happens in one basic shot. One small victory for the camera in its history of losses against the motor car.

Later we do a shot which aptly illustrates the divine madness of photography, particularly inside a moving car. The shot is a locked-off camera inside the front seat of a period taxi, on Boland, Collins and de Valera, as they drive away from Lincoln prison. The taxi has a black leather hood, with a tiny oval, two inches by six, maybe, through which the streets outside can be seen behind the actors' heads. Chris Menges has illuminated an entire city block around which the taxi will be towed, to fill that tiny sliver that will be seen at the back of the screen. Also, of course, to light the actor's faces. His concentration on everything that goes into the image is extraordinary—as are the situations in which we sometimes end up. His eye is like George Washington. It cannot tell a lie. So we sometimes enact the most false and artificial events in order to guarantee the documentary integrity of the image.

Sunday 24th September

Another Sunday, another open crowd-call. The Bloody Sunday massacres, where a convoy of Black and Tans invaded Croke Park football grounds and opened fire on the crowds, have embedded themselves in folk memory. We have invaded Carlisle soccer grounds in Bray, which for many years was my home, and re-created Croke Park. We have rehearsed the action on Saturday with Pat Clayton and his army of stuntmen. The scene calls for crowds crawling over barricades, running in terror from machine-gun fire and the possibility of serious injury is real. Each stuntman will have to marshal one hundred extras.

While the crowds gather outside, we shoot the football game. Two Gaelic teams wearing caps, and period shorts down to their knees. I suppose it functions like light relief before what's to come, and the camera crews are enjoying themselves, trying to outdo each other in the way they anticipate the movement of the ball.

After lunch the crowd is in place and it is some sight. Three sides of period stands jam-packed with people, all in perfect period gear. We shoot the convoy bursting through the gates, wheeling on to the pitch while the game is in full flow and coming to a half in the middle. Then we rest the cameras for the main event.

The main shot is a track around the armoured vehicle, which will begin the gunfire. It has two machine-gun barrels pointing out of its tin pot, one aimed at the left stand, one at the right. So it should begin with the east stand in view, the gun firing off west and end with the west stand in view, the other gun coming into frame, firing off east. Four other cameras are positioned round the pitch and stands, all hopefully out of view of each other. The cameras roll and the mayhem begins. The machine-guns rattle, the crowd ducks, screams, tries to hide at first, then as the Black and Tans ringing the pitch begin to fire, the crowds scatter, over the barricades, across the pitch, fleeing one area of gunfire to encounter another. It must be the folk memory of the event that makes them react so well. Or else Pat Clayton has outdone himself. Maybe a combination of both. Anyway, it works like a terrifying dream. When the guns—and the stands—are empty, we call cut.

When the dust settles, we find there is one injury, a young teenage girl who panicked in the crush. Oddly enough, she turns out to be Michael Collins's grand-niece. An ambulance comes on and it emerges she's in a state of shock but with no bones broken. We decide to go with the one take, shoot a few small inserts and repair to the Harbour Bar, where the atmosphere is like the day Ireland beat Italy in the World Cup.

Monday 25th September

After the Croke Park massacre, the Treaty Debates. The reading-room at Trinity College doubles for the National

University. A journalist from an English paper asks me about the relevance of today's scene to events in the Peace Process. I tell her she should go up the road to where the Sinn Fein Ardheis is being held as we speak and compare the two events. She tells me she's too busy.

The scene as written is composed entirely of quoted dialogue. From the speeches of Cathal Brugha, Eamon de Valera, Arthur Griffith, Michael Collins. The debates took place over twenty-nine days and we have had to squeeze them into one. My worry is that the language of the records is slightly stilted, as if the Irish legislature was wrestling for the first time with parliamentese. But once the cameras start rolling and the blood is up, it takes on its own life. Gerry McSorley, playing Cathal Brugha with a wonderful vituperative vindictiveness, the soul of the betrayed Republic now exacting its revenge. Collins enters through the upper level and descends into this bear-pit that the Dail has become. Harry Boland, now on the opposite side of the chamber, unable to look at him.

Michael D. Higgins, the minister for Arts and Culture drops by and seems amused by it all. Maybe he's seen enough of politics to take this with a pinch of salt.

Alan Rickman has pored over Dev's speeches and added some lines to what I had written. After the vote is cast and his side is narrowly defeated, Alan rises to his feet and delivers his protest. It seems too long, and the stilted dialogue of the period seems to be crushing the meaning of what he is saying. Or the very personal tragedy of the event. I ask him to deliver it as if he doesn't know, until the words come out, what he is about to say. And he does it. How, I don't know, but one has the impression of an earth-shattering decision being taken in mid-speech, that is made almost before he is aware of it. After the speech he gets up,

leaves the chamber. One by one his deputies follow. Liam
rises to his feet and again quotes Collins. Taitors all. He
somehow makes the archaism of the phrase work. Aidan
sits stunned, as Harry Boland, then finally rises to his feet
and passes Liam. Not you, Harry—another quote. Again, I
think acting is the most mysterious business of all.

Tuesday 26th September

Out to Hollywood, Co. Wicklow, to the road we have built
through the small glacial valley which will serve as Beal na
mBlath. We are coming to the end of the film and will end,
appropriately enough, with Collins's death. Being practically minded I suppose, I dive right into the thing itself.
The fact that the road was purpose-built for it makes the
whole orchestration of the scene remarkably easy. Mike
Roberts sits with a hand-held camera in the front seat of
the touring car. Collins sits in the back beside Joe O'Reilly,
ruminating about who he'll invite to his wedding. The convoy turns a corner, is stopped by a road-block—and the
entourage spills out on to the road to shift it. Mike pans
with Collins as he strides forwards to find out what the
problem is.

  We set up a track then, alongside the convoy as the firing begins. Collins striding forward, to find out how long
the blockage will take, when a shot ricochets off the armoured vehicle behind him. He stares up into the heights,
screams in fury as he and his party take cover and begin to
return fire. A machine-gun jams, Joe O'Reilly leaps to get it
working, rakes the hill, 'cutting the briars off the ditches'
as someone said, and Collins behind him momentarily

leaves his covering vehicle. Takes a bullet in the head and goes down. We cover it several times, with two cameras, then as the light fades, we place the camera behind the prone figure of Liam. Joe O'Reilly empties his machine-gun into the hillside above him, turns to Mick, exhilarated at having beaten them off, and discovers the worst. He leaps down to the grass, holds the bleeding head of his boss and pleads desperately, as if his words could bring him back to life. And he realises they won't.

When the light has faded and we finish shooting, though, the actors are stunned. It seems to them almost too peremptory, too casual. I try to explain that that is how it was, a casual bullet in an ambush that felled him while nobody was watching; that any glorious death, in the manner of *Platoon*, say, would be inappropriate. Then I get worried myself. We retire to the pub in Hollywood and the discussion about the scene continues. Ian Hart, who plays O'Reilly, seems upset, though he is too gracious to say it. Liam is plagued by nagging doubts about whether it will satisfy an audience. I explain how the scene was designed to be intercut with the shots of Julia Roberts being fitted for her wedding dress, and feel like the shabbiest of directors, claiming it will all work out in the cutting-room. I realise gradually that what is upsetting everybody is that the film is ending and that, quite understandably, nobody wants it to stop. There is always a slough of despond when a film is over, which one tries to resist but which creeps up regardless. And in an experience as intense as this one, the crash will be doubly felt. The shooting moved so quickly that no one had time to second-guess themselves. But now all they will have is time—time to wonder did I do that right, could I have said that line differently, etc.

Wednesday 27th September

I have managed to squeeze a helicopter from the production for a series of shots that will show the group of ambushers running over the heather towards the heights, then reveal the sweeping valley below, with the convoy snaking through it. The wind is whipping up dangerously, and while waiting for the chopper to arrive I shoot some cover on yesterday's scenes and we have our first serious accident. The shots involve the ambushers taking up position round a statue on the heights above us. One of them falls through the heather, into a hidden chasm and nobody can get to him. The scene for a while is truly horrible. Screams of panic from above, ADs trying to climb the inaccessible rocks from below to reach him. We call an emergency helicopter from the military airport nearby and manage to get him out, on to a stretcher, shot with painkillers, as comfortable as he can be. Then, while we are waiting for the emergency chopper to arrive, I begin shooting again. My daughter, Sarah, who is working as a PA and is unused to the callous practicality of a film unit, berates me for being heartless. I try to explain to her that our activity or inactivity down here below won't make the cavalry arrive sooner, so to speak. Mike Roberts smiles wryly, sitting on the dolly, and tells her he fully expects to croak it in mid-shot some day and for the next take to begin while his body's still warm. Then the chopper does arrive, the stuntman is winched up from the heather and we are told by radio that he is fine. A man of incredible fitness, his muscularity saved his back from being broken by the fall.

The winds are howling by now and our own chopper has arrived, complete with its Westcam camera mount. The pilot, an Irishman with experience in Vietnam, decides to give it a go, though the vortex the winds are creating above the valley make it extremely dangerous. I go up with them and take them through the shot, bouncing around the skies like a puppet whose strings are about to snap. The shot is spectacular, and the problem as always is trying to get the aircraft low enough, within the margins of safety. Most of these unit helicopter pilots have brief lives and, being up there with him, I can understand why. The extras down below only have so much running in them, particularly after the accident. Leaping over mounds of heather, at full speed, with a helicopter trying to breathe down your neck in a force 9 gale is not the best way to earn your living. After several takes, everyone gives up from exhaustion, and I can feel the film is truly winding itself down.

Friday 17th November

Have now seen the finished film three times. The first time, since we are using an electronic editing system called Lightworks, which give a dim pixillated image, was like coming up for air. Or like the inhabitants of Plato's cave, emerging to see with their own eyes what they had previously seen as shadows on the wall. Chris Menges' photography is extraordinary on the big screen. Some action on the sides of the frame that I had forgotten existed. The movement of the story, though, is too logical. The progression of events to much like a historical chronology—and then . . . and then . . . and then . . . But any worries about the picture falling into two halves, of the battleground of the first half making the tragedy of the second half seem like a downer were put to rest. The second half, in general, was better than the first. If only because by the time an hour was spent and the Truce was declared, one knew the characters and the issues, and was no longer straining to keep up with the events. But one thing in particular that came through was the power of the acting. And the relief that with the fireworks on display from all of the players, Liam strode through it like a colossus.

The second viewing had not entirely solved the problems of the first half, but the dilemmas and the antagonisms were clearer. With that came a concern that the violence of the events could either alienate the audience from Liam's character or become in a weird sick way a celebration.

On the third viewing the logic and the forward movement of the first half is just right. And I realise that there is something about either the character of Michael Collins or Liam's portrayal of him that makes him impossible to dislike, whatever the horror of the events he sets in motion. In fact, the reverse could rather alarmingly be true. You admire him for his ruthlessness. And I remember the conversation I had with Liam all those months ago in Skibbereen.

So, the arguments about Irish politics that this film will give rise to, spurious or no, will run something like this:

—that it's a statement in support of violence as a means to achieve a political end.

—it's a misrepresentation of Britain's relationship with Ireland and its place within the Empire at the time.

—it's a one-sided portrayal of a period in Irish political history that had more gradations of grey than black and white. One that never shares the point-of-view of those in this country whose sympathies were with the Empire, etc.

—that the events portrayed in the first half have a broadly republican slant and imply that violence can work as a means towards a political end.

—that the events portrayed in the second half would seem to support The Treaty, and by implication, Partition.

—that one never shares the point of view of those in the country who's sympathies were with the Empire.

To all of which I've only one reply. That I told the story from the point of view of the protagonists themselves; showing their aims, methods and politics from their perspective; and showed the havoc that these wreaked upon them in the end.

Sunday 31st January 1996

A piece of brazen stirring in the *Sunday Times,* with a Headline to the effect that my film is about to wreck the Peace Process. A list of presumed historical inaccuracies, quotes from a slew of Irish historians—Roy Foster, Ruth Dudley Edwards, Tom Garvan and the head of the United Unionist party, David Trimble. All commenting on a film they haven't seen. The first time I've been thrashed for a movie I've not even finished. I would have thought historians would know better than to comment on something they have no access to. And that Trimble would have more to do with his time, given the current state of things. But since he has refused to talk to Sinn Fein, the SDLP and the Irish Government, maybe he is suffering from a dearth of conversation.

The next morning I'm asked to go on Irish radio with

Roy Foster, who holds a chair of History at Oxford and is Yeats's biographer. I say I'll speak if I can talk to Foster directly, since I'm intrigued by the thought of an historian who seems not to bother with primary sources. And by a biographer of Yeats who doesn't seem to care for the inter-action of imagination, politics and history. The conversa-tion gets nowhere, predictably. If anything he seems a little embarrassed.

Tuesday 9th January

Preview in Pasadena, California, of all places. Everyone from the studio is there, with David Geffen. The audience are almost too attentive. Nobody moves for two hours. But when we come towards the end, I realise this audience have no prior knowledge of the character, and, more impor-tant, don't know he has to die. I remember what Stanley Kubrick said some years ago when he read the script: you have to tell them at the start that he dies, otherwise they'll think he goes on to become President of Ireland and will be disappointed. Stanley, being American, knows that au-dience and that you must address them as if addressing a blank page. And the way I've choreographed the ending depends on that knowledge, for even the satisfaction of knowing you can weep. When the lights come up there is considerable applause. Terry Semel, Bob Daly and the War-ners people seem to be thrilled. But I'm worried that the preview audience were more respectful of the film than moved by it.

Wednesday 10th January

We have the studio meeting after the preview, where the cards the audience filled in are assessed. Or should I call it the autopsy? But from the enthusiasm around the table at Warners, it's obvious they have got something far bigger than they had anticipated, and potentially more commercial. David has problems with the editing, which I already know about, and feels we have to see Julia learn about Collins's death. At the moment the film cuts from his death to a bridal wreath being placed around her head in the wedding shop. And in the great European tradition, emotion is implied rather than presented. We agree on some limited extra shooting—that scene plus a prelude and a coda which I will come up with.

Thursday 8th February

In New York, for the additional photography, as all the actors are here. Tony Pratt has re-created a series of Dublin interiors in a large mansion in Dobb's Ferry, outside Manhattan. I have written the two 'bookending' scenes, involving Joe O'Reilly talking to Kitty Kiernan after Collins's death, a scene where Kitty, returning from the wedding shop is told the bad news by a young officer, and two additional scenes to deepen the love-triangle.

The first scene to be shot is with Julia and Aidan. She reads a letter from Mick in London, and when Boland makes a romantic move towards her, she rebuffs him. Tells him she is in love with Mick. We had gone through the scene the day before without the actors, and changed the blocking from what was written. When the actors rehearse we change it again, back to basically what it was before. Which only goes to show that (1) actors imagine the scene as written, and (2) it is pointless to attempt to prejudge what they will do.

Aidan and Julia were particularly good together. This is

the scene they probably imagined behind all the scenes they played, but that I had hitherto denied them.

Then the scene where Julia enters Liam's office and a gunman fires at them through the window. 'I'm going to live to see you old.' 'Till your hair turns grey.' 'I come from a long line of baldies.' Dangerously romantic. But we manage to get realism into it. What is remarkable is how easily they all step back into the skins of their characters, in these odd surroundings, months after the shoot.

For the penultimate scene: she walks up the hotel stairs. She comes to the landing. We see the soldier behind her on the opposite balcony but she doesn't. She walks the length of the balcony and, when she turns the corner, stops. She sees him now. He stops too. She sees his tear-stained face. She turns away. She says, 'No—No—don't tell me.' He tries to hold her. She struggles free and runs down the stairway . . .

Friday 9th February

Shoot the above, which turns out great. Then the bridging scenes with Joe and Kitty. At the end he walks into her bedroom, pulls back the curtains to let the light in and draws her to her feet. Chris is worried about them being silhouetted against the windows, with no light on their faces. I tell him those silhouettes have been his signature throughout the film, it's too late to worry about them now. Anyway, they are marvellous.

After we finish the reshoot we hear about the London bombing, at Canary Wharf, and the breakdown of the ceasefire. Everyone is depressed and subdued. I'm reminded of Stephen Rea's aside to me while shooting. He meets me outside his caravan and says, Neil, I'm worried. I say, what about. He says, you promised Warners there'd be no more war if they made this movie. And it's not looking hopeful.

Meet Stephen Rea, Terry George (the writer of the film *In the Name of the Father*), Elliott Goldenthal (the composer), among others, in Moran's Pub in Manhattan. A very Irish night ensues. The kind of political discussion that comes out of upset. Oddly, the movie is like a prism that reflects every development of the recent situation. Even the lines in the letter-scene we shot. 'They couldn't defeat us by force of arms but now I swear they're trying to defeat us by force of verbiage.'

Building up to a preview on Thursday, which makes me physically ill.

The next day, very hungover from the night before, viewing the dailies and fitting them into the picture. Doing ADR (Audio Dialogue Replacement) with Stephen (Rea). I always find him inexplicably moving, in whatever part he plays. Not only in his performance, but in his commitment to the film as a whole. He serves it. He makes you feel thoughts, on the screen. I walk down with him to the street. Broadway. I say, will you do *The Butcher Boy?* He says, when? I say, June. He says, yes. That simple.

Thursday 15th February

Preview in New York. Irish and Irish American crowd. The cards show 90 per cent approval of the film, which seems to be unprecedented, from what Warners tell me. David Geffen there, very excited. Plus a plethora of stars—Julia, Liam, Brad Pitt, Gwyneth Paltrau, Vanessa Redgrave, all hiding in obscurity in the back. Vanessa comes out after the screening, profoundly moved, actually weeping. Have a party of sorts afterwards and it feels like a première. So the cut must be finished.

MICHAEL COLLINS

Author's Note

It goes without saying that a screenplay is just an outline for a film that one hopes will be made some day. This one was first written in 1982 and went through numerous changes between then and now. In other words it changed in all its details, yet remained exactly the same. What is published here is the final version, with the various major rewrites that I felt were necessary through the shooting included. I have not adjusted the text to take account of all the day to day changes that occur during the shooting of a movie—snatches of dialogue, improvisations, scene and location descriptions, etc.

CAST

(in order of appearance)

Joe O'Reilly	IAN HART
Kitty Kiernan	JULIA ROBERTS
British Officer	RICHARD INGRAM
Michael Collins	LIAM NEESON
Harry Boland	AIDAN QUINN
Patrick Pearse	JOHN KENNY
Thomas McDonagh	RONAN MCCAIRBRE
Thomas Clarke	GER O'LEARY
James Connolly	MICHAEL DWYER
Captain Lee-Wilson	MARTIN MURPHY
Eamon de Valera	ALAN RICKMAN
Smith	SEAN MCGINLEY
Hoey	GARY WHELAN
Kavanagh	FRANK O'SULLIVAN
Ned Broy	STEPHEN REA
Sean McKeoin	FRANK LAVERTY
Rory O'Connor	OWEN O'NEILL
Tom Cullen	STUART GRAHAM
Liam Tobin	BRENDAN GLEESON
Cathal Brugha	GERARD MCSORLEY
Austin Stack	LIAM D'STAIC
Arthur Griffith	OWEN ROE
Cosgrave	PAUL BENNETT
Vaughan's Hotel Clerk	CLAUDE CLANCY
Dublin Castle Soldier	PAUL HICKEY
Vinny Byrne	TOM MURPHY
Charlie Dalton	DAVID GORRY
Squad Youth #1	GARY LYDON
Squad Youth #2	DAVID WILMOT

Squad Man #1	JOE HANLEY
Squad Man #2	COLM COOGAN
Chaplain at Lincoln Jail	AIDEN GRENNELL
Lincoln Taxi Driver	DAVE SEYMOUR
Belfast Detective	IAN MCELHINNEY
Soldier on Station	TONY CLARKIN
Soames	CHARLES DANCE
McCrae	LUKE HAYDEN
Black and Tans on Lorry	GARY POWELL
	MAX HAFLER
Rosie	LAURA BRENNAN
Gresham Hotel Bellboy	AIDAN KELLY
Man following Broy	JIM ISHERWOOD
Black and Tan	MICHAEL JAMES FORD
Officer in Bath	MAL WHYTE
Officer in Bed	MARTIN PHILLIPS
Girl in Bed	AISLING O'SULLIVAN
Officer in Park	MALCOLM DOUGLAS
Croke Park Hurler	BRIAN 'JOKER' MULVEY
Tenor in Restaurant	FRANK PATTERSON
Pianist in Restaurant	PETER O'BRIAN
Orchestra in Restaurant	CAFE ORCHESTRA
Journalist	MIKE MCCABE
Speaker in the Dail	VINNIE MCCABE
Vice-Consul McCready	ALAN STANFORD
Young Gunman	GARY PAUL MULLEN
Free State Soldier	BARRY BARNES
Republican #1	DENIS CONWAY
Republican #2	DON WYCHERLEY
Santry the Blacksmith	PÁRAIC BREATHNACH
Drinker in Pub	TERRY WOODS
Collins' Assassin	JONATHAN RHYS MYERS

1. INT. DARK ROOM. DAY

JOE O'REILLY *sits in a darkened room. He speaks almost directly to the camera with a strange intensity.*

JOE: You've got to think of him. The way he was. The way he fought the British without one ounce of hatred. The way he'd cycle round Dublin in his pin-striped suit, with ten thousand pounds on his head. Why hide, Joe, he'd say, when that's what they expect? And he never did what anyone expected. Some people have greatness flowing through them. They're what the times demanded. And life without them seems impossible. But he's dead. And life is possible. He made it possible.

[*Then the film begins*]

2. EXT. GENERAL POST OFFICE. DAY

A bullet-shredded tricolour—the flag of the Irish Republic— hanging out of an upper window. The window explodes as a shell hits it.

A caption reads: DUBLIN 1916

3. INT. GENERAL POST OFFICE. DAY

COLLINS, *in his early twenties, screaming wordlessly, his head pressed against a wall as the shell crashes through the window next to him, leaving it in ruins. When the smoke clears, he whips round, fires rapidly out of the window, then ducks again as bullets ricochet through it.*

4. EXT. O'CONNELL STREET. DAY

Camera pulls back to reveal O'Connell Street, shrouded in smoke. Massive guns boom, off, and more shells explode through the roof of the General Post Office. It is ringed by groups of British soldiers, crouched behind sandbags, burning cars, overturned carts. Behind them masses of Dubliners stare, as if at a carnival.

5. EXT. O'CONNELL STREET. DAY

A massive shell hits the Post Office roof, sending masonry crashing to the pavement below, shrouding the building in smoke and dust. As the smoke clears, we catch a glimpse of a white flag, a man in a makeshift uniform holding it. Behind him are other members of the Irish Republican Army, bleeding, tattered, exhausted. They stand there as the smoke clears, staring at the carnage around them. Camera isolates COLLINS, *the last of them, and the youngest. Baby-faced and tough, his eyes totally impassive. Beside him is* HARRY BOLAND, *the same age, looking more shaken.*

COLLINS: The game's over Harry. Lost again . . .

   [*He raises his hands behind his head, in an attitude of surrender.* BOLAND *does likewise.*]

6. EXT. HOSPITAL LAWNS. DAY

The Republicans are lined up against the railings, in full view of the Dublin streets. COLLINS *and* BOLAND, *their arms over their* heads, shuffle forwards. COLLINS *bumps into one of the leaders, the tall, imposing figures of* EAMON DE VALERA.

COLLINS: So they got the Long Fella too . . .

DE VALERA: They did, Michael.

COLLINS: Fucking Greek Tragedy that was—

DE VALERA: We proclaimed the Irish Republic.

COLLINS: But did anybody listen, Dev?

[*He looks around him. Sees:*
A mass of Dubliners press their faces through the railings. A line of British soldiers face them, their guns at the ready. CAPTAIN LEE-WILSON, *a British officer, walks down the lines with a group of Dublin detectives in plain clothes—*SMITH, REDMOND, HOEY *and* KAVANAGH, *and the youngest of them,* BROY.]

LEE-WILSON: Now show me the ringleaders of this little farce . . .

[SMITH *a stocky, brutal specimen in a trenchcoat does the dirty work—with a riding-crop.*]

SMITH: Pearse—with the gunner eye.

[SMITH *lashes* PEARSE *across the cheek. The soldiers drag him from the line. The group moves on down.*]

SMITH: McDonagh . . .

[*He points. The soldiers drag* MCDONAGH *out.*]

[SMITH *comes closer to* BOLAND, COLLINS *and* DE VALERA. *Next to* COLLINS *is a badly-wounded older man, bleeding from the shoulder, with a drooping moustache.* SMITH *prods his shoulder with the crop.*]

SMITH: Connolly . . .

[*The soldiers drag* CONNOLLY *forward.* CONNOLLY *collapses on the grass.* SMITH *kicks him till he rises.*]

SMITH: Get up, you Fenian swine, get up—

[COLLINS *goes to move from the line.* DE VALERA *restrains him.*]

DE VALERA [*Whispers*] Wait, Michael. Wait.

COLLINS: Till when?

DE VALERA: Till the next time.

[SMITH *moves past* COLLINS *and* BOLAND, *who move not a facial muscle as the eyes glance over them.*]

SMITH: De Valera—

[*He prods* DE VALERA *with his crop, who is dragged off. The condemned* LEADERS *are dragged up towards a line of soldiers. A British officer with a monocle proceeds to strip them naked. Nurses leaning out of the upper hospital windows begin to cheer and hoot.*
BOLAND *says, ironically, to* COLLINS:]

BOLAND: What happens next time?

COLLINS: We won't play by their rules, Harry. We'll invent our own.

[COLLINS *watches as the naked men are forced through a line of soldiers, who kick them and prod them with bayonets. His face is expressionless.*]

7. EXT. KILMAINHAM YARD. DAY

SMITH *and the Irish detectives stand by the jail entrance.* SMITH *taps the door with his crop. The door opens and* PEARSE *is taken out.*

PEARSE *is marched to a wall, blindfolded. We hear orders, off, and bullets pummel through him.*

A group of soldiers, in an execution square. They reload.

8. INT. KILMAINHAM CELL. DAY

The shots echo through the cell. A figue at a table, unresponsive to the shots, writing. It is DE VALERA.

DE VALERA: [*Voiceover*] The fact that I was born in America might save my hide. Either way I am ready for what comes.

9. EXT. KILMAINHAM YARD. DAY

SMITH *and the Irish detectives stand by the jail entrance.* SMITH *taps the door with his crop. The door opens and* MCDONAGH *is taken out.* MCDONAGH, *blindfolded by the wall. Orders, off.* MCDONAGH *is shot.*

10. INT. KILMAINHAM CELL. DAY

The terrible echo of the shots again. DE VALERA *is still writing.*

DE VALERA: [*Voiceover*] The Irish Republic is a dream no longer. It is daily sealed by the lifeblood of those who proclaimed it. And every one of us they shoot brings more people to our side . . .

11. EXT. KILMAINHAM YARD. DAY

SMITH *taps the door once more.* CONNOLLY, *half-dead now, is carried out, in a chair, by several soldiers.*

The chair, with CONNOLLY, *in it, is placed by the wall.* CONNOLLY *is shot.*

12. INT. KILMAINHAM CELL. DAY

DE VALERA, *still writing.*

DE VALERA: [*Voiceover*] They cannot imprison us for ever. And from the day of our release, Michael, we must act as if the Republic is a fact. We defeat the British Empire by ignoring it . . .

13. EXT. KILMAINHAM JAIL. DAY

A wide panorama of Kilmainham Jail, with the city seen behind it. The bark of orders is heard, and another volley of shots. The empty streets are ringed by soldiers.

14. EXT. DUBLIN CASTLE. DAY

The centrepiece of British power in Ireland—a granite, barred mausoleum in the city's centre. The street towards it is ringed by British soldiers and all the pavements are strung with barbed wire. Frightened faces peep out of curtained windows. A lone child scurries past the soldiers as a group of military vehicles trundles down the street, carrying the detectives and officers, their business with the executions finished.

15. EXT. COUNTRYSIDE. DAY

A train moves through the Irish countryside on a hot summer's day.

A caption reads: IRELAND 1918.

16. INT. TRAIN. DAY

COLLINS *and* BOLAND *are sleeping in a carriage. They are dressed in cheap businessmen's suits, and could be brothers—one tough and burly, the other slim and fine-boned.*

A fly settles on COLLINS's *nose. His hand automatically brushes it off—and wakes him up in doing so. He sighs, glares at the carriage around him, then at* BOLAND. *He kicks gently at the sole of* BOLAND's *shoe.*

COLLINS: They let us out, Harry, so we can do our best to be put inside again.

[BOLAND *sleeps.*]

COLLINS: Don't you see a certain paradox in that?

[BOLAND *doesn't respond.* COLLINS *reaches forward and knocks off his hat.*]

COLLINS: Paradox, Harry. A contradiction. Where an immovable force meets an immovable object kind of thing—

[*Still* BOLAND *doesn't move. Then* COLLINS *leaps on him.* BOLAND, *as if expecting the assault, swings his body sideways and grips* COLLINS *round the neck.*]

BOLAND: You're the bloody paradox—

[*The wrestle like two schoolboys and crash against the door, falling through it.*]

17. EXT. SMALL STATION. DAY

A BRIDAL PARTY *is on the platform as the train pulls in. The* BRIDE, *clutching her veil, is obscured by the billowing steam.* COLLINS *and* BOLAND *emerge,* BOLAND *with his hand to his ear.* COLLINS *sees the* BRIDE *emerge from the steam like a wraith.*

COLLINS: Maybe we should settle down.

BOLAND: Just the two of us.

COLLINS: And him.

[COLLINS *nods towards the station exit, where* BROY, *one of the detectives of the opening sequence, can be seen. There is a car, with two men at the wheel, which can be glimpsed through the entrance, past the detective.*]

COLLINS: Let's go.

[*He walks straight past* BROY, *without glancing at him.* BO-LAND *follows. They both pile into the car.*]

18. INT. CAR. DAY

The car tears down small country lanes in a cloud of dust, avoiding geese, chickens, etc. Every tree along the road is festooned with election posters, showing a man in prison uniform. SEAN MCKEOIN, *a local Volunteer, a burly blacksmith, is driving.* COLLINS *peers through the back seat at a car which is following.* BROY *is at the wheel, with another detective beside him.*

COLLINS: How did they know we were coming?

MCKEOIN: They know what we eat for breakfast.

COLLINS: There's only one way we'll beat them then. Find out what they eat for breakfast—

[MCKEOIN *swerves down a small side road, bumps dangerously along it, then whips rapidly down an even smaller one. He almost crashes into a herd of cattle, being driven in single file by a farmer. He screeches to a halt. The detective's car, following, almost crashes into their rear.*]

COLLINS: Fuck—

MCKEOIN: It's market day.

[*Neither cattle nor car can move forward on the small road,* COLLINS *gets out. He walks to the detective's car, and bangs on the window.*]

COLLINS: So, what did you have for breakfast?

[BROY *says nothing.*]

COLLINS: Bit of a traffic jam here. If you backed up then we could back up and you could chase us some more.

[BROY, *still saying nothing, goes into reverse.* MCKEOIN: *does likewise, and the cattle begin to pass through.* COLLINS *gets into the front car.*]

COLLINS: On your marks, get set, go—

[*The car screeches off. The other car follows.*]

19. EXT. GRANARD, DAY

A massive crowd in the square of a small market town. Herds of horses and cattle mingle with the people. COLLINS *is standing on the back of a lorry at one end, giving a speech. Behind him are posters of a man in prison uniform, and a slogan: PUT HIM IN TO GET HIM OUT.*

The car is parked across the square. BROY *sits inside, taking notes.*

COLLINS: The fact that the candidate you're being asked to vote for is at the moment rotting in an English jail shouldn't put you off. I was in one myself till a week ago.

[*He is a rough, impassioned speaker, but tremendously power-ful—he speaks the same language as all the rough, tough peas-*

ant farmers around. We see the effect of his words on their faces.]

COLLINS: They can jail us. They can shoot us. They can even conscript us. They can use us as cannon-fodder in the Somme. But we've got a weapon more powerful than any in the whole arsenal of their British Empire.

[*He pauses dramatically.*]

COLLINS: And that weapon is our refusal. Our refusal to bow to any order but our own. Any institutions but our own.

[BOLAND *stands beneath the lorry with a group of tough-looking* VOLUNTEERS, *all holding hurleys.* MCKEOIN *nudges his arm and points to beyond the group . . . where we can see the dark uniforms of the* ROYAL IRISH CONSTABULARY *gathering.*]

BOLAND: Don't let them touch him.

[BROY *leans against the car, at the back of the crowd, taking notes, with another* DETECTIVE. *All around him, we can see the* ROYAL IRISH CONSTABULARY *drawing their batons. He glances from them to* COLLINS—*and his expression tells us nothing. We can hear* COLLINS*'s voice above the crowd.*]

COLLINS: Our friends in the Royal Irish Constabulary would like to shut me up. Jail me again. Shoot me, who knows. But I'd like you to send them a message. If they shut me up, who'll take my place?

[*Every hand in the market place punches into the air.* COLLINS*'s face is obscured by the sea of hands. We still hear his voice.*]

COLLINS: WILL THEY SHUT YOU UP?

[*The* CROWD *roars*—NO!
The CONSTABULARY *charge.*
The CROWD *breaks into mayhem, some fighting, some fleeing in terror.*

A TINKER *leaps on a horse and rears it towards a group of onrushing* CONSTABULARY. *They cut through the crowd, smacking heads, trampling women and children. The crush around the platform becomes unbearable.* BOLAND, MCKEOIN *and the* VOLUNTEERS *push through it with their hurleys, fighting the* CONSTABULARY *off.* MCKEOIN *himself is like a tiger, unstoppable.* BOLAND *swings his hurley and sends a police helmet flying.* COLLINS *screams from the platform but not a word can be heard.*

A *baton flies through the air and glances off his forehead, drawing blood. He falls into the crowd, the* CONSTABULARY *try to reach him but the* CROWD *beats them back, inch by inch . . .*

At *the back of it all,* BROY *stares, some strange detachment in his eyes.*]

20. INT. HOTEL. NIGHT

COLLINS *lifts his head from a bowl of water. A girl's hand lays a cloth over the wound on his forehead.* COLLINS *opens his eyes. He is looking into the face of* KITTY KIERNAN, *a local girl.*

COLLINS: What's your name?

KITTY: Kitty. And don't move.

COLLINS: Is Harry here too?

KITTY: Downstairs. What did they hit you with?

COLLINS: Whatever it was it was hard.

KITTY: You'll be all right then . . .

COLLINS: You a nurse, Kitty?

KITTY: I'm nothing. I'm my father's daughter.

COLLINS: And who's your father?

KITTY: He's dead.

[*She moves away from him, towards the door.*]

KITTY: There'll be dinner in an hour, if you fancy it.

[*She smiles at him nervously, then leaves.* COLLINS *rises. He grimaces, holds his head, then looks in a mirror. He runs his hand through his hair, and begins straightening his collar.*]

21. INT. DINING ROOM. NIGHT

KITTY *sings a song by the piano, in the formal way of those days. There are five daughters in all, and they sit ranged around the living room, in a strange, quite beautiful tableau.* COLLINS *listens, a glass of sherry in front of him, on his best behaviour.*

KITTY: 'My young love said to me my brothers won't mind
And my parents won't chide you for your lack of kind
And she moved away from me and this she did say
It will not be long, love, till our wedding day . . .'

[*When the song finishes, his eyes are moist.* BOLAND *looks at him.*]

BOLAND: Mick's going to make a speech.

COLLINS: It's beautiful.

BOLAND: What did I tell you.

COLLINS: Ah what would you know about singing, you Dublin jackass you—

BOLAND: I agree. You're the expert in singing. So it's Mick's turn now.

COLLINS: Give over, Harry. She's a voice like an angel, I've one like a goat.

BOLAND: Ladies, is it or is it not Mick's turn?

KITTY: A noble call is mine and I call on Mick.

BOLAND: Come on, Mick. Your party-piece.

[COLLINS *stands, under persuasion by the party. He glowers at* BOLAND, *throws his head back and begins to recite.*]

COLLINS: 'Oh well do I remember the bleak December day,
The landlord and the Sheriff came to drive us all away;
They set my roof on fire with their cursed English spleen
And that's another reason why I left old Skibbereen . . .'

22. INT. BEDROOM. MORNING

COLLINS *and* BOLAND *lie asleep in the same small bed, both dangling out of opposite ends. We can glimpse a revolver under* COL-LINS's *pillow. The door opens slowly and* KITTY *comes in.* COLLINS *opens one eye, watching her. She walks to the window and pulls back the blinds. Sunlight streams through the room. She glances at the bed and sees that* COLLINS *is awake. He doesn't move.*

KITTY: You wanted to be woken.

COLLINS: There was a man in West Cork proposed to five sisters, one after the other—

KITTY: I suppose they all refused.

COLLINS: Then the father died so he proposed to the mother.

KITTY: Are you trying to tell me something?

COLLINS: I was building up to a proposal. But it's not easy with a Fenian in your bed.

[*She walks over to him. He takes her hand.*]

COLLINS: He likes you too.

KITTY: Stop it now.

COLLINS: But he snores.

BOLAND: [*Waking*] No I don't.

COLLINS: So it's up to you, Kitty—

KITTY: I don't have to like either.

COLLINS: That's true.

[*He kicks* BOLAND *out of the bed and on to the floor.*]

COLLINS: And he sleeps in his trousers . . .

23. INT. MCKEOIN'S FORGE. DAY

A forge in the early morning with the coals still burning from the night before. COLLINS *and* BOLAND, MCKEOIN *and a group of* IRA VOLUNTEERS. *They are all very young, but rugged and tough-looking, dressed in threadbare clothes, some of them barefoot.* COLLINS, *as usual, takes the centre of the floor.*

COLLINS: We'll be an invisible army. Our uniform will be that of the man in the street, the peasant in the field. We'll come out of a crowd, strike the enemy and vanish into the crowd again.

[ERNIE O'MALLEY, *a young volunteer, speaks up.*]

O'MALLEY: What do you propose we strike with?

COLLINS: Show us what you've got . . .

[*Handfuls of rusty old weapons are extracted from their jackets and thrown on the stone floor.* COLLINS *examines them.*]

COLLINS: Same old story. You need something better. And there's only one place to get it. Sean—

[MCKEOIN *takes a crumpled handwritten map from his pocket and unravels it.* COLLINS *points to it.*]

COLLINS: The RIC barracks. There's an arsenal in there—

O'MALLEY: How do we get in? We haven't even got bullets—

COLLINS: But they don't know that—

[*He takes up a sode of turf from near the fire.*]

COLLINS: What's that?

O'MALLEY: Sod of turf.

COLLINS: Wrong. That's a weapon. Fucking deadly.

[*There is a ripple of laughter among them.* COLLINS *smiles.*]

COLLINS: You don't believe me.

[COLLINS *takes a metal hook and slams it through the sod of turf. He dips it in a nearby bucket full of petrol, then ignites it from the fire. The sod blazes.*]

24. EXT. RIC STATION. NIGHT

Masses of blazing sods are flung through the air. The roof of the station catches fire. VOLUNTEERS *stand around it with their empty weapons trained on the door.* RIC MEN *come out coughing, guns in hand.*

COLLINS *rises from behind the* VOLUNTEERS. *Addresses the RIC men.*

COLLINS: Gentlemen. We're relieving you of your responsi-
bilities . . .

[*The* RIC MEN *see the guns pointed at them and drop their own.*]

25. INT. RIC STATION. NIGHT

COLLINS, BOLAND *and the* VOLUNTEERS *flood through the door, opening cases. Rifles spill all over the floor.*

COLLINS: Jaysus, lads. It's Christmas—

[BOLAND *begins to stuff rifles into two large holdalls.*]

26. INT. SCHOOLROOM. DAY

COLLINS *and* BOLAND *with a new group of recruits.* COLLINS *opens the holdalls.*

COLLINS: You'll be organised in flying columns. You'll live
on the run. You'll engage the enemy on nobody's terms
but your own.

[*He hands out rifles.*]

COLLINS: I want each one of these to capture ten more. And
I want you to account for every bullet.

27. INT. TRAIN. DAY

COLLINS *and* BOLAND *travelling. Fires burning in the countryside beyond the window.*

28. EXT. PUBLIC HOUSE AND STREET. NIGHT

COLLINS *walks rapidly down an empty Dublin street.* JOE O'REILLY, *a small, comically nervous man is running alongside him, trying to keep up.*

COLLINS: Am I late, Joe?

O'REILLY: Not yet.

COLLINS: Won't do to keep the government waiting.

[*He abruptly plunges through a public house door.*]

29. INT. PUBLIC HOUSE. NIGHT

COLLINS *enters and walks rapidly to the end of the pub, where several men are waiting with* BOLAND. COLLINS *takes a notepad out of his boot.*

COLLINS: I want some details before we go in, Harry—

BOLAND: Hang on.

[*He points to the bar, near the door. There is a man sitting on his own there, nursing a pint. We recognise* BROY, *one of the detectives who was following them in the first scenes.*]

COLLINS: Jesus wept.

[*He considers for a moment, then rises just as abruptly as he entered. He walks to the end of the bar, past* BROY, *giving him a hard glance as he does so. Then he walks back out of the pub.*]

30. EXT. PUBLIC HOUSE. NIGHT

COLLINS *ploughs through the door, then ducks down a little alley-way behind the pub, out of sight. After a moment,* BROY *emerges.*

BROY *looks around the empty street for a moment, then begins to walk. A hand comes out of the darkness, grabs him by the scruff of the neck and drags him down the alleyway. It is* COLLINS, *who puts a gun at* BROY's *neck.*

COLLINS: So what is it?

[BROY *looks from* COLLINS's *face to the gun. He says nothing.*]

COLLINS: You've been on my heels for weeks now. Very fucking eager for a G-man.

BROY: I've something for you.

[COLLINS *takes the gun from his neck.* BROY *reaches for his pocket.* COLLINS *tenses again.*]

COLLINS: Don't—

BROY: Don't you ever calm down?

[*He takes a list from his pocket. He hands it to* COLLINS.]

BROY: Names and addresses of the whole cabinet. They're to be lifted tonight.

[COLLINS *studies the list.*]

BROY: It's an illegal gathering. In open defiance of His Majesty's Government.

COLLINS: How'd you get this?

BROY: Like you said. I'm eager, for a G-man.

COLLINS: Why should I trust you?

BROY: Logically I suppose you shouldn't. But as you said, I've been on your heels for weeks. Making notes of your speeches. Let's just say you can be persuasive.

COLLINS: You work for the Castle, for Jaysus' sake.

BROY: I know. What was it you said? Our only weapon is our refusal—

[COLLINS *can't believe what he's hearing. He shakes his head.*]

COLLINS: What's your name?

BROY: Broy. Ned Broy.

COLLINS: A queer bloody G-man.

BROY: Take it or leave it . . .

[*He walks off.* COLLINS *watches him go, then slowly goes back into the pub.*]

31. INT. CATACOMBS. NIGHT

Camera tracks through a vast cavernous series of cellars beneath a brewer's to reveal the illegal Irish government in sitting. Seated round the dominating figure of DE VALERA *are* ARTHUR GRIFFITH, AUSTIN STACK, COLLINS, BOLAND *and others—all members of the illegal cabinet. An argument is in progress, between* COLLINS *and* CATHAL BRUGHA, *a small waspish Republican, veteran of many years' struggle.*

BRUGHA: The minister is as usual exceeding his brief.

COLLINS: And just what is my brief, Cathal?

BRUGHA: Intelligence.

COLLINS: Bullshit. I'm minister for gun-running, daylight robbery and general mayhem. Until we get the boys armed, nothing will happen.

[*He looks at* BRUGHA *mischievously.*]

COLLINS: But, as minister for intelligence, I'd like to inform you that every man-jack of us is to be arrested tonight.

[*Silence falls over the gathering.*]

BRUGHA: How does the minister know this?

COLLINS: The minister was told this by a G-man.

BRUGHA: By what G-man?

COLLINS: Don't ask me that, Cathal. He was putting his neck on the line as it is.

[*He takes out the list and hands it to* DE VALERA.]

COLLINS: Names, addresses, next of kin. They know more about us than our mothers do.

DE VALERA: How do we know it's genuine?

COLLINS: We don't. But it could be. So don't sleep at home tonight.

[DE VALERA *looks down the list and considers.*]

DE VALERA: I disagree. Do sleep at home tonight. If Mr. Collins has been gulled, we'll sleep soundly. If not, they will arrest the cabinet. The public outcry will be deafening. Maybe then the world will listen.

[COLLINS *is aghast.*]

COLLINS: Dev, Dev, you can't be serious. We've been rotting in English jails for long enough . . .

DE VALERA: I am serious, Michael. But it's only my opinion. Why don't we put it to the vote.

[*He raises his hand. As does the rest of the gathering, but for* COLLINS *and* BOLAND.]

32. EXT. STREETS. NIGHT

COLLINS *cycles through the night streets with* BOLAND.

COLLINS: Fuck them.

BOLAND: Watch your tongue.

COLLINS: I will in future.

[*The sudden sound of lorries. Blazing headlights illuminate the streets.* COLLINS *pulls* BOLAND *into the shadows.*]

COLLINS: See what I mean—

[*A group of lorries whizzes by, filled with soldiers.*]

COLLINS: Come on—

[*He jumps on his bike and cycles after them.*]

33. EXT. CATHAL BRUGHA'S HOUSE. NIGHT

A working-class street of cottages. The lorries tear into view and screech to a halt. BOLAND *and* COLLINS *are cycling behind the last one, at breakneck pace. Crowds gather, as the* SOLDIERS *run from the lorries to* BRUGHA's *house, batter down the door and drag him out.* COLLINS *and* BOLAND *merge with the crowd, watching the scene. The lorries roar off again.* COLLINS *and* BOLAND *follow as before.*

34. EXT. HOUSE BY SEA. NIGHT

A row of bungalows by the sea. DE VALERA *is being led from his doorway to one of the lorries by the* SOLDIERS. *He walks with unmistakable dignity. A small crowd is watching. He stops and addresses them.*

DE VALERA: This is an illegal arrest by an illegal force of occupation—

[*He is dragged into a lorry. A near riot ensues as the lorries
drive off.* COLLINS *and* BOLAND *cycle up as the lorry pulls off.
They can see* DE VALERA'*s face in the back window.*]

COLLINS: Jesus Christ.

BOLAND: So what does the minister think?

COLLINS: Which minister?

BOLAND: We're the only two left . . .

COLLINS: I'm changing your brief, Harry. I hereby appoint
you the minister for general mayhem.

BOLAND: And what's your brief:

COLLINS: The same. Plus one other portfolio. Jailbreaks.

[*He pushes his bike towards de Valera's house.*]

COLLINS: It's the safest house in Dublin now. May as well
stay the night . . .

35. INT. SINN FEIN BANK—COLLINS'S OFFICE. DAY

COLLINS *sits in his office. He lifts the phone and dials.*

COLLINS: Inspector Broy, please.

[*Pause.*]

COLLINS: Tell him it's John Grace.

36. INT. PUBLIC LIBRARY. DAY

BROY *enters a public library, obviously looking for someone. All he
sees is a group of quiet readers, the gleam of table-lamps. He wan-*

ders among the shelves, and bumps into a figure there, between them. It is COLLINS, *a book open in his hands.*

COLLINS: So what's your game, Mr. Broy?

BROY: Don't have a game.

COLLINS: Why'd you give me that list?

BROY: Why didn't you act on it?

COLLINS: I did. But the cabinet thinks it's more useful in jail.

BROY: You obviously don't agree.

COLLINS: No, I don't—

[*He suddenly turns* BROY *to face him.*]

COLLINS: Look—all I know is you're from the Castle. And the Castle spies and informers run us through like woodworm.

BROY: You could play the same game.

[COLLINS *looks into his eyes.*]

COLLINS: A queer bloody G-man.

BROY: I hate them. I hate what I do.

[BROY *looks at* COLLINS *who is still suspicious.*]

BROY: You don't believe me, do you?

COLLINS: I'm not sure . . .

BROY: What would it take to convince you?

[COLLINS *ponders a moment. Then he snaps his book shut.*]

COLLINS: You could show me the Castle files.

BROY: I'd never get them out.

COLLINS: No. But you could get me in.

[BROY *can't believe what he is hearing.*]

BROY: My God . . . you're serious . . .

COLLINS: You think I'm joking?

[COLLINS *has decided to trust him, though. He becomes practical.*]

COLLINS: Does anybody know what I look like?

BROY: Only me.

COLLINS: Pretend I'm a grass. Let me in around midnight.

BROY: And you think I'll get away with it?

COLLINS: Everything's possible, if you wish hard enough. Now who said that?

BROY: You did.

COLLINS: No. It was him.

[*He points to the book he is holding. We see an illustration of Peter Pan.*]

37. EXT. STREET—NEAR CASTLE. NIGHT

COLLINS *cycles through the city. Ahead of him, the dark shape of Dublin Castle looms out of the mists. He slows as he approaches the massive gates. Two* SOLDIERS *stand guard.* COLLINS *steps off his bike and approaches them.*

COLLINS: Howya.

[*The* SOLDIERS *eye him.*]

COLLINS: Grand evening.

SOLDIER: Not bad.

COLLINS: Broy here?

SOLDIER: Broy who?

COLLINS: Detective Ned Broy. Told me to drop by if I'd any information . . .

SOLDIER: You want G wing?

[COLLINS *nods. The* SOLDIER *looks him up and down, then frisks him.*]

COLLINS: Might rain, though.

SOLDIER: You think so?

COLLINS: Then again, maybe not.

[*The* SOLDIER *gestures him through.*
    COLLINS *wheels his bike through the gates, into the cobble-stoned courtyard. The place seems terrifying. He takes a deep breath and moves forward.*]

38. INT. CASTLE. NIGHT

A stone staircase. COLLINS *walks up it as a* SOLDIER *comes down.* COLLINS *taps his hat, shielding his face, as he passes. Then takes a deep breath and moves on.*

A gloomy corridor, lit by gas-lamps. Two burly MEN *in shirt-sleeves, with guns and shoulder-holsters, are walking down it.* COLLINS *is walking down the corridor, sees them, and can't turn back. He walks forward, passes them unchallenged. As they round the corner, he heads for a large door marked 'G DIVISION'.*

    COLLINS*'s hand on the door. He hesitates. Then suddenly the* *door is pulled open for him. He finds himself face to face with* SMITH, *the brutal detective in the opening sequence.* SMITH *has a sheaf of papers in his hand.*

COLLINS: Detective Broy?

[SMITH *shakes his head. He point to a door behind him.*]

SMITH: Third on the left—

[COLLINS *touches his cap obsequiously and walks past him.*]

39. INT. BROY'S ROOM. NIGHT

BROY *sits at his desk. A clock on the wall reads midnight. A rapid tap on the door. He goes to it.*

BROY: Who is it?

COLLINS: Grace, sir. John Grace.

[BROY *opens the door.* COLLINS *steps through.* COLLINS *keeps up the act.*]

COLLINS: Begging your pardon, sir, but I've some information on a certain party—

BROY: Who?

COLLINS: A right bousy, sir, the lowest of the low, a gutter-snipe called Collins—

[BROY *closes the door.* COLLINS *grins.*]

BROY: You're not nervous?

COLLINS: I'm shaking. Where's the record-room?

[BROY *walks ahead to another door, opens it, leads him to a*

*smaller corridor. There is an RIC guard there, asleep at a small
table, a bottle of whiskey beside him.*]

COLLINS: Yours?

[BROY *nods.* COLLINS *takes the bottle, drinks from it.*]

COLLINS: I'll pay you back.

BROY: Don't bother.

[*He takes the key from the desk by the RIC man. He opens a
door to a room filled with cabinets, with a small barred
window.*]

BROY: I have to lock you in. If you hear anyone outside,
don't make a sound.

[COLLINS *takes a deep breath.*]

COLLINS: Game ball.

BROY: And if you're caught, you're on your own.

COLLINS: Don't I know it.

[COLLINS *enters the room.* BROY *closes the door behind him.*]

40. INT. RECORD-ROOM. NIGHT

The door clangs shut behind him. The key turns, locking him in.
COLLINS *looks round the room for another exit, sees none. He goes
to the barred window and pulls on it. It is solid. He is in a sealed
tomb.*

COLLINS: Jesus wept.

[*He takes another breath, takes out a notebook and goes to
work on the files.*]

41. EXT. CORRIDOR. NIGHT

BROY *walks past the sleeping guard. He paces down the corridor slowly, then goes to his room.*

42. INT. RECORD-ROOM. NIGHT

A shelf of documents. COLLINS*'s hand flicks through them. We see lists of guerrilla leaders, politicians, etc. He scribbles down notes as he goes.*

43. INT. BROY'S ROOM. NIGHT

The clock ticks on. An hour has passed. BROY *sits at his desk, twisting a pencil in his hand, obviously nervous. He hears a commotion in the corridor, and runs for the door.*

44. INT. CORRIDOR. NIGHT

HOEY *the detective, is trying to wake the drunken* POLICEMAN.

HOEY: Christ, that's all we need—get up, you drunken bousy . . .

[BROY *comes forward.*]

BROY: He was celebrating, Tom. The birth of his child.

HOEY: What was it? Boy or girl?

[*He rummages around the desk. Takes out the record-room keys.* BROY *goes pale.*]

BROY: A girl . . .

[HOEY *walks to the door. Puts a key in. It jams, won't turn.*]

45. INT. RECORD-ROOM. NIGHT

COLLINS, *hearing the key in the door, looks around in panic.*

46. EXT. RECORD-ROOM. NIGHT

BROY *grabs the whiskey bottle and walks towards* HOEY.

BROY: Have a drink, Tom. All work and no play—

[*The key turns. The door swings open.* HOEY *walks in.* BROY *stands ashen at the door.*]

47. INT. RECORD-ROOM. NIGHT

HOEY *walks to the shelves of files. There is no sign of Collins. He takes a file from the shelf.*

48. EXT. RECORD-ROOM. NIGHT

BROY, *looking in. He can see* COLLINS *suspended from the ceiling, hanging from the barred skylight, sweat pouring from him with the effort not to fall.* HOEY *walks out again, below him, holding the file. He closes the door and locks it.*

HOEY: A drink, is it?

[BROY *pours out the whiskey with a shaking hand.*]

49. INT. RECORD-ROOM. NIGHT

COLLINS *falls to the ground like a cat. He immediately goes back to work, flicking through the files. He comes upon a photograph of himself. He smiles, pockets it.*

50. INT. CORRIDOR. NIGHT

HOEY *finishes his drink, stands. Looks at the half-empty bottle.*

HOEY: Shame to let it go to waste.

BROY: Take it with you.

> [BROY *hands him the bottle.* HOEY *walks off, swinging from the neck.*]

51. INT. RECORD-ROOM. DAWN

Weak threads of sunlight coming throught the window. COLLINS *still working away, looking exhausted. The door opens quietly.* BROY *enters.*

BROY: Time to go, Mick.

COLLINS: Wait a minute.

> [*He keeps flicking through the files.* BROY *pulls him away.*]

BROY: Mick, Mick, you're pushing it.

> [BROY *pulls him from the room.*]

COLLINS: Can you get a typist on your side?

BROY: I could try.

COLLINS: I want every new file copied, and sent to me.

BROY: I'll try, Mick. Now you've got to leave.

> [*He leads him past the still sleeping policeman, and into his room.*]

52. INT. BROY'S ROOM. DAWN

COLLINS: You could squash us in a week, you know that?

BROY: We could.

COLLINS: If we don't get there first. Things might have to get rough.

BROY: How rough?

COLLINS: Very rough. Those files are no good without the G-men who compiled them. If we get rid of the G-men . . .

BROY: That's rough all right.

COLLINS: Could you stand it?

BROY: After tonight, I'll stand anything.

[COLLINS *hits him on the shoulder and is gone.*]

53. EXT. CITY STREETS. MORNING

COLLINS *cycles through the empty streets along the Liffey. Mist all around.*

54. INT. SINN FEIN BANK—COLLINS'S OFFICE. DAY

COLLINS *lies slumped over his desk, in the empty office. Footsteps on the stairs, and* CULLEN *enters, with* O'REILLY *in tow.*

O'REILLY: Jesus Christ—where have you been?

COLLINS: Working.

O'REILLY: Working where?

[COLLINS *says nothing.* O'REILLY *shouts.*]

O'REILLY: You have to tell us things, Mick. We thought they had you in the Castle—

COLLINS: They had.

[*He rises, bleary-eyed.*]

COLLINS: I want a file drawn up on every member of the British administration. Look through whatever you can find—*Who's Who, Stubbs,* society columns—give me names, addresses, clubs, where they bank down to what they eat for breakfast—and keep it up to date—add to it every week.

[*He gestures to* CULLEN.]

COLLINS: Seamus—get me a list of the twelve best men in the Dublin division. Young, without families—

CULLEN: For what—

COLLINS: The Twelve Apostles—just do it, would you, for fuck's sake—and, Joe—

[*He turns back to* O'REILLY.]

COLLINS: Take a letter.

[*He begins to dictate.*
The door burst open and BOLAND *enters.*]

BOLAND: Where the hell have you been?

[COLLINS *doesn't answer. He continues dictating.*]

COLLINS: Any further collaboration with the forces of occupation will be punishable by death. You have been warned. Signed, The Irish Republican Army.

[BOLAND *can't believe his ears.* COLLINS *yawns and rubs his eyes.*]

BOLAND: You're serious.

COLLINS: Afraid so.

Michael Collins and Harry Boland both vied for the affections
of Kitty Kiernan. The rupture in their relationship mirrored
the wider rupture in the country at large.
(Photo by Tom Collins)

Liam Neeson as Michael Collins
(Photo by Tom Collins)

Aidan Quinn as
Harry Boland
(Photo by Tom Collins)

Stephen Rea as Ned Broy
(Photo by David James)

Alan Rickman as
Eamon de Valera
(Photo by Tom Collins)

Michael Collins urges rural voters to support the nationalist movement in the 1918 election. *(Photo by Tom Collins)*

Michael Collins defending the G.P.O. (General Post Office) during the failed 1916 rising. *(Photo by Tom Collins)*

As arguments over the treaty spread, the country lurches toward civil war. *(Photo by Tom Collins)*

The surrender of the 1916 insurgents to the British Forces outside the G.P.O. *(Photo by Tom Collins)*

Michael Collins' assassin in wait at Beal Na Blath. *(Photo by David James)*

Neil Jordan (writer, director) directing Liam Neeson in the surrender of Dublin Castle. The British flag comes down as the Irish flag ascends. *(Photo by David James)*

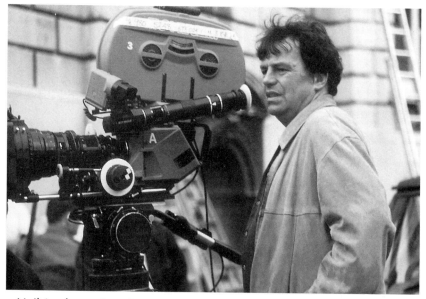

Neil Jordan *(Photo by Tom Collins)*

Irish director Jim Sheridan with Neil Jordan on set in front of the
G.P.O. *(Photo by Tom Collins)*

Focus puller Alan Butler (left), camera operator Mike Roberts,
and Neil Jordan *(Photo by Tom Collins)*

Harry Boland and Michael Collins worked toward the same nationalistic goal until they differed over the terms of the treaty that separated the six counties of the north.
(Photo by Tom Collins)

Kitty Kiernan at a pro-treaty rally in her hometown, Granard.
(Photo by Tom Colllins)

Kitty and Harry share a dance.
(Photo by Tom Collins)

[BOLAND *shakes his head.*]

COLLINS: Send one to every G-man.

[COLLINS *slumps back on his desk, exhausted.*]

COLLINS: I had a look at their files. They know more about us than we do.

[*He looks up at* BOLAND.]

COLLINS: That's how serious I am.

[*He reaches into his pocket, takes out two photographs. One of himself, the other of Boland.*]

COLLINS: That's us . . .

[*He tears them into shreds.*]

COLLINS: You know how they survive, don't you?

BOLAND: Spies. Informers.

COLLINS: Without them there'd be no system. They couldn't move. Now, imagine Dublin with the Castle like an enclave—where anyone, and I mean anyone, who collaborated knew he'd be shot. They wouldn't be able to move outside those walls.

BOLAND: There's only one problem.

COLLINS: What's that?

BOLAND: You'd have to do it.

COLLINS: Yes.

[*He stares at* BOLAND.]

COLLINS: Could you bear it?

BOLAND: You know I could. It's you I'm worried about.

[*He stands.*]

BOLAND: I've got to go, Mick. I'm late.

COLLINS: For what?

BOLAND: Just late.

[BOLAND *rises and goes.* COLLINS *looks at the scraps of photo-graphs on the floor.*]

55. EXT. STREET. DAY

COLLINS *walks down the crowded street. Past British* SOLDIERS, *lunchtime crowds, etc. At the corner of the street is a fountain—and at the fountain he sees* BOLAND *with* KITTY. *They do not see him.*

  COLLINS *watches them turn and walk through the crowds. He follows. He sees from behind* BOLAND'S *arm slip round* KITTY'S *waist. He comes so close behind them he is almost breathing down their necks. He speaks into* KITTY'S *ear.*

COLLINS: Didn't I tell you he snores . . . ?

KITTY: Jesus—

[*She turns.*]

COLLINS: God, you're lovelier than ever—

[BOLAND *turns and is obviously embarrassed.*]

BOLAND: You remember Kitty, Mick—

COLLINS: Yes. But does she remember me?

[KITTY *is as embarrassed as* BOLAND. COLLINS *raises his arms.*]

COLLINS: All right—I'm going. Know when I'm not
   wanted—

56. INT. VAUGHAN'S HOTEL ROOM. NIGHT

COLLINS *is sleeping in one bed,* O'REILLY *in the other.* BOLAND *enters
silently, doing his best to wake nobody.* COLLINS *opens one eye,
which follows him round the room.*

COLLINS: I'll wrestle you for her.

BOLAND: She wouldn't be interested. A bogman like you—

COLLINS: Want to bet?

   [*He jumps on* BOLAND. *They wrestle like demented children.*
   O'REILLY *sleeps on blissfully through it.*]

57. INT. THEATRE. NIGHT

An empty theatre. Armed VOLUNTEERS *guard the exits. The camera
pans round the empty auditorium, to the stage, to where a group
of* YOUNG MEN *stand among abandoned theatrical scenery and flats.
They are mainly working-class, very young, members of what will
become Collins's 'Squad'.* COLLINS, BOLAND, O'REILLY *and* CULLEN
sit across from them. COLLINS *talks.*

COLLINS: Any of you who have read Irish history will know
   that movements like ours have always been destroyed
   by paid spies and informers. And I want to set up an
   outfit that will rectify that. Your job will be to wreck
   the system of information the Castle uses against us. To
   make it unhealthy for them to run it.

   [VINNY BYRNE, *one of the Squad, speaks up.*]

BYRNE: How unhealthy?

COLLINS: I've sent letters of warning to every G-man. If they stay in the Castle, they'll be shot. You'll have to do the shooting.

[*Pause.*]

COLLINS: Don't expect it to be pleasant.

[*Pause.*]

COLLINS: And anyone who has qualms better leave now.

[*Pause. No one moves.* VINNY BYRNE *pipes up.*]

BYRNE: Would they have got past the door?

[*The tension in the air is dispersed by laughter. And we see now how young the* MEN *really are.* COLLINS *shakes his head.*]

COLLINS: They would have, Vinny. I won't force this on anyone.

58. INT. BROY'S OFFICE. DAY

BROY *opens his mail. The first letter he reads is the death threat. INSERT—the* LETTER:

'Any further collaboration with the forces of occupation will be punishable by death. You have been warned. Signed, The Irish Republican Army.'

Through the door comes SMITH, *smashing it open, kicking over a filing cabinet. His irascible little face is lit bright red with anger and he has the letter in his hand.*

SMITH: You got one, too?

BROY: It's a joke.

SMITH: No Fenian guttersnipe threatens me—

[*He kicks the files at his feet.*]

SMITH: Give us a name, Ned—

BROY: What for?

SMITH: Someone to hang up and fry like bacon—

[*He grabs a handful of files at random.*]

SMITH: Here's one—Cullen . . .

59. EXT. SINN FEIN BANK AND STREET. DAY

COLLINS, *cycling through the streets, turns a corner towards his office. He finds* O'REILLY *running towards him.*

O'REILLY: Make yourself scarce, Mick—

[O'REILLY *grabs the handlebars.* COLLINS *slips off the bike, leaving* O'REILLY *holding it. There is a crowd of people gathered round a police van.* COLLINS *walks casually towards them.*

    He sees CULLEN *being dragged down the steps towards the police van.* CULLEN *collapses, and* HOEY *kicks him towards the van door. The crowd stares,* COLLINS *among them.* HOEY *lifts* CULLEN *off the ground.*]

CULLEN: *You're for it, Hoey—*

HOEY: *No, you are—*

[CULLEN *is thrown bodily inside. The van drives off.* COLLINS *watches it go, as* O'REILLY *comes up behind him.*]

O'REILLY: What happens now, Mick?

[COLLINS *says nothing, staring at the departing van.*]

60. INT. CASTLE. DAY

CULLEN *is dragged down one of the Castle corridors.* BROY *stands at his doorway, watching him pass.*

61. INT. HOEY'S ROOM. DAY.

SMITH, KAVANAGH *and* HOEY *stands there as* CULLEN *is pulled in* HOEY *grabs* CULLEN *and throws him against a filing cabinet.*

HOEY: You don't threaten us, you Fenian swine

[CULLEN *stands.* HOEY *comes towards him and hits him again.*]

HOEY: We're the ones that threaten you—

[SMITH *grabs the letter from the table, and holds it up to* CULLEN'S *face.*]

SMITH: What does this mean—

CULLEN: It means you can get out now—

[HOEY *hits him with a chair.* CULLEN *falls to the floor, spitting blood.*]

HOEY: What? Give up my job? Miss out on all the fun?

CULLEN: Or face the music, Hoey—

[SMITH *kicks him on the floor.*]

SMITH: You're the only one'll make music here, boy—

62. EXT. HOEY'S ROOM. DAY

BROY *in the corridor, hearing the cacophony inside.*

63. INT. SINN FEIN BANK. NIGHT

COLLINS, BOLAND *and* O'REILLY *pace around the wreckage of their office after the raid.* COLLINS *kicks a chair across the room. It almost hits* BOLAND, *who is sitting on the other side.*

BOLAND: Watch it—

COLLINS: Sorry—

[*The telephone rings.* O'REILLY *jumps for it.*]

O'REILLY: Yeah—

[*He holds the receiver to* COLLINS.]

O'REILLY: For you.

[COLLINS *takes it.*]

COLLINS: Yes—Ned—

[*He listens. Then puts the phone down.*]

COLLINS: They've dumped him.

[*They make for the door.*]

64. EXT. BRUNSWICK STREET. NIGHT

CULLEN *leans against a shop-front window in the empty late-night street. His face is bleeding, badly beaten. A car screeches to a halt beside him and* COLLINS *gets out with* O'REILLY.

COLLINS: Tom—

CULLEN: Hoey . . .

COLLINS: I know. Don't talk—

[*He helps* CULLEN *towards the car.*]

65. INT. CHURCH. MORNING

VINNY BYRNE *in a half-empty church, praying. He blesses himself carefully, then rises.*

66. EXT. MARKET. MORNING

HOEY, *the detective, walking through a busy fruit market on his way to work. A figure comes behind him, on a bicycle. We recognise* VINNY BYRNE.

BYRNE: May the Lord have mercy on your soul, Hoey—

[HOEY *turns, puzzled. He looks from* BYRNE'*s intent face, down to the handlebars of the bike. He sees a gun in* BYRNE'*s hand. For a moment he can't believe it. Then* BYRNE *shoots, several times. As* HOEY *falls, he cycles furiously through the screaming crowds.*]

67. INT. LINCOLN JAIL. MORNING

A Host, raised by a CHAPLAIN'*s hand.*

CHAPLAIN: Hic est enim corpus meum—

[*We are in a sacristy in the prison. Irish* PRISONERS *sit in the pews, dressed in prison uniform.* DE VALERA *is serving beside the priest, his tall gaunt form dressed in a white altar-boy surplice.*
    The CHAPLAIN *raises the chalice. A pair of keys can be seen beneath his surplice.*]

68. INT. VESTRY. DAY

The CHAPLAIN *is disrobing. He leaves the belt with the keys dangling over a chair.* DE VALERA *washes the cruets.*

CHAPLAIN: I want to thank you.

DE VALERA: For what, Father?

CHAPLAIN: For these mornings we've prayed together.

[*He swills the remains of the wine in the chalice and drinks it.*]

CHAPLAIN: I can't pretend to understand your politics. But I can appreciate your integrity.

DE VALERA: And I yours.

[*The* CHAPLAIN *goes into an ante-room,* DE VALERA *takes a candle and presses one of the keys from his belt into it, so the candle acts as a mould. He slips the candle under his surplice, as the* CHAPLAIN *emerges again.*]

CHAPLAIN: And if prayer can transcend these things, there's hope, surely.

DE VALERA: There must be.

69. EXT. FURNITURE SHOP. DAY

A tender screams to a halt outside another of COLLINS'*s offices.* SOLDIERS *pile out—*KAVANAGH, SMITH, BROY, *and other G-men with them.*

70. INT. FURNITURE SHOP—COLLINS'S OFFICE. DAY

Chaos, as COLLINS'*s staff try to leave, grabbing files and bringing them with them.* COLLINS *scatters petrol round the room from a can. He throws a match and the room explodes into flame.*

71. INT. FURNITURE SHOP—STAIRWAY. DAY

One of the Squad shoots at the troops coming up the stairs. They return fire, hitting him several times.

72. INT. FURNITURE SHOP—LANDING. DAY

COLLINS *runs from the burning room, clambers up to a skylight and out on to the roof.*

73. EXT. FURNITURE SHOP—ROOFTOP. DAY

COLLINS *clambers between the valleys of the roof. He comes to another skylight, lifts it and drops in.*

74. INT. CLERK'S OFFICE. DAY

COLLINS *drops into a roomful of ledgers. There is an* OLD CLERK *sitting at a desk. He looks up, surprised.*

COLLINS: Shhh . . .

[*The* CLERK *stares at him.*]

COLLINS: How do I get out of here?

[*The* CLERK *points to the door.*]

75. EXT. FURNITURE SHOP. DAY

COLLINS *emerges from the building adjacent to what used to be his offices. There are crowds staring at the* SOLDIERS, *the smoke pouring from the upstairs window, etc.* COLLINS *presses through the crowd and sees members of his staff being bundled into the tender . . .*

76. EXT. CHURCH. DAY

Crowds, emerging from Sunday Mass. KAVANAGH, *the detective, comes out with them.* TWO YOUTHS *are standing there behind paper-stands.* KAVANAGH *stops, reaches in his pocket for coins.*

KAVANAGH: Give us a *Mail*, would you—

[*Bullets suddenly explode from beneath the paper-stands, peppering* KAVANAGH.]

YOUTH: For the job on Friday.

[*They shoot him, many times.* KAVANAGH *falls. The crowds scream and run in different directions.*]

77. INT. ABATTOIR. DAY

COLLINS *strides through a busy abattoir with a handkerchief to his nose.* O'REILLY *runs behind him.*

COLLINS: Are these the best premises you could get me, Joe? A knacker's yard?

O'REILLY: Just a temporary stop-gap, Mick, I swear to God—

COLLINS: And where then? The city morgue?

[O'REILLY *opens the door and ushers him into a small office.*]

78. INT. ABATTOIR OFFICE. DAY

The two SQUAD YOUTHS *who shot Kavanagh are lounging on the office table reading the paper. There is a parcel wrapped in brown paper on the table beside them. As* COLLINS *opens it one of the* YOUTHS *pipes up.*

YOUTH 1: Made the front page, Mick.

COLLINS: So what does it say?

YOUTH 2: Castle Detective riddled with bullets.

COLLINS: Riddled! What are you going round riddling people for! Ten or twenty bullets when the one would do!

YOUTH I: We just wanted to be sure he wouldn't get up but—

COLLINS: Lads—just try to remember they don't grow on trees, all right?

[*He turns abruptly away from them. He examines the candle.*]

COLLINS: When did this come in, Joe?

O'REILLY: This morning.

[COLLINS *turns.*]

COLLINS: You did well, boys. But go easy on the riddlin'—

[*They leave. Then he turns back to* O'REILLY.]

COLLINS: And you're sure it's from Dev?

[O'REILLY *nods.*]

COLLINS: Pure genius.

79. EXT. IRISH SEA. EVENING

A ship. Crossing the Irish Sea.

80. EXT. SHIP'S DECK. EVENING

COLLINS, BOLAND *and* TOBIN *are on the upper deck of a ship, pitching through the Irish Sea.*

BOLAND: Don't you ever want a wife to come home to? A brace of snotty-nosed kids by the fire? Ordinary things, you know? Peace and quiet. Instead of this—

COLLINS: This what?

BOLAND: This bloody mayhem.

COLLINS: Yeah, I want peace and quiet. I want it so much I'd die for it.

BOLAND: You'd kill for it first.

COLLINS: No, not first. Last. After centuries of trying to talk reason. After years of parliamentary chicanery. After every other road has been exhausted. After they've made it clearer than the daylight that you've no alternative.

[BOLAND *smokes and deals.*]

BOLAND: Did it ever strike you you were good at it?

COLLINS: Good at what?

BOLAND: Bloody mayhem.

COLLINS: You're not so bad yourself.

BOLAND: I mean more than good. I mean you leave them sitting in the halfpenny place.

[*A disturbance in the air after* BOLAND's *words.* COLLINS *stares at the water.*]

COLLINS: We haven't seen anything yet.

BOLAND: So we've got to be even better.

COLLINS: Yes. And do you know what I think then? I hate them. Not for their race. Not for their brutality. I hate them because they've left us no way out. I hate whoever put a gun in young Ned Tannin's hand. I know it's me, and I hate myself for it. And I hate them so much that I have to do that. I hate them for making hate necessary. And I'll do what I have to to end it.

81. EXT. LINCOLN JAIL. NIGHT

A line of prostitutes stand in the shadow of the jail wall, plying their trade.

By the roadside, a cab is parked with its engine running. TOBIN *sits in the cab, the barrel of a gun held to the temple of the terrified* CABBIE.

At the corner of the jail wall BOLAND *stands, like any punter eyeing up the prostitutes.*

A light flashes on in an upper window of the jail.

TOBIN, *from whose vantage point the light can be seen, cocks the trigger of the gun.*

TOBIN: Flash your headlights once.

> [*The sweating* CABBIE *obeys.*
>
> BOLAND, *by the wall's corner, strikes a match and lights a cigarette.*
>
> COLLINS, *many yards beyond the corner, by the other, isolated section of the wall, sees the flare of Boland's match. He is standing by a metal-barred door. He taps on the door with a large metal key. Whispers.*]

COLLINS: Two minutes to the next watch, Dev—

> [*He inserts the key gingerly into the lock. Turns it. We hear a dull snap.*]

COLLINS: Fuck's sake—

DE VALERA: [*Off*] Mind your language—

COLLINS: Dev—the bleedin' key broke—

DE VALERA: [*Off*] I'll try mine—

COLLINS: You can't—the keyhole's fucking jammed—

DE VALERA: [*Off*] That's no excuse for obscenities—

[*We hear the scraping of metal.*]

DE VALERA: [*Off*] Maybe I can force it out . . .

[*And amazingly, with agonising slowness, we see the broken portion of the key emerge. Then slowly, with what seems a deafening creak, the door opens.* DE VALERA *is revealed, shivering in prison uniform.*]

COLLINS: Man, but you're blessed.

[*He takes a woman's fur coat from the ground and wraps it round* DE VALERA'S *shoulders.*]

DE VALERA: What's this?

COLLINS: Your fur coat. Pretend you're a tart.

[*He takes* DE VALERA'S *arm and begins to walk, rapidly.*]

DE VALERA: Michael—

COLLINS: What, my sweet?

[*They reach* BOLAND. BOLAND *takes* DE VALERA'S *other arm.*]

BOLAND: Fancy a cuddle, love?

DE VALERA: Whose idea was this?

[*As they pass some tarts, a klaxon begins to shriek from the prison.* COLLINS *and* BOLAND *break into a run, across the grass towards the car.*]

DE VALERA: All I'm missing is the high heels—

[*They pile into the cab.*]

82. EXT/INT. CAR. NIGHT

TOBIN *is in the front seat, with the gun to the* CABBIE'S *head. The others pile in the back. A light swings towards them from the prison. There is the sound of dogs barking.*

TOBIN: Drive, would you—

[*The* CABBIE *is nervous and the car shakes with his revving.*]

TOBIN: Easy—

CABBIE: You try being easy with that thing in your ear—

[TOBIN *swings his shoulder against the driver, pushing him out of the door and on to the street. He switches seats then, pulling off with a screech of rubber. On the roadside, the* CABBIE *shields his eyes from the glare of the spotlight.*]

83. INT. CAR. LATER

TOBIN *drives, bearing the leader of the Irish Nation into the night, still wrapped in the fur.*

COLLINS: You look good in furs, Chief—

DE VALERA: There are certain things one shouldn't do for one's country—

BOLAND: Like go on the game?

[*The begin to hoot with laughter.*]

COLLINS: Some died for Ireland. But Dev—he tarted for Ireland—

DE VALERA: I suppose it does set a historical precedent.

COLLINS: 'I'll take you home again, Kathleen . . .'

[COLLINS *hugs him, out of genuine relief.*]

DE VALERA: I see you've been having fun in my absence.

BOLAND: Oh fun and games all the way, Chief.

DE VALERA: I know. I read the papers.

[DEV *isn't laughing now. But no one seems to notice.*]

84. EXT. LIVERPOOL DOCKS. DAY

COLLINS *walks with* BOLAND *towards a news-stand. Every headline announces Dev's escape.*

COLLINS: Mother of God. We're famous.

BOLAND: No, he is.

[COLLINS *buys a paper, then walks out of the paper-seller's earshot.*]

COLLINS: Better lie low for a week. That nose of his is hard to hide. Then the whole of Dublin can throw a hooley. And what then, Harry?

BOLAND: America.

COLLINS: *What?*

BOLAND: He wants to go to America. And he wants me to go with him . . .

85. INT. SAFE HOUSE IN LIVERPOOL. DAY

DE VALERA , TOBIN, KERR *sitting.* COLLINS *strides in with* BOLAND, *agitated.*

COLLINS: Dev—you can't do this to me—

DE VALERA: I want to petition the American public for their support. I want recognition from President Wilson for an Irish Republic. I want the moral force of international opinion brought to bear on the British government.

COLLINS: There's only one kind of force they understand and you know it. Our job is at home—

DE VALERA: Our job is where I say it is. And as president of the Irish Republic I want recognition from the President of the United States.

COLLINS: You won't get it.

[*Silence falls.* DE VALERA *looks at him icily.*]

DE VALERA: Let me be the best judge of that.

COLLINS: Go on to America, blast you. But leave me Harry.

DE VALERA: What's so special about Harry?

COLLINS: I know my men. And I can't do it without him.

DE VALERA: Do what?

COLLINS: I can't run a war without him.

DE VALERA: You could run it without me . . .

[COLLINS *looks to* BOLAND. BOLAND *says nothing.*]

86. EXT. O'CONNELL STREET. DAY

DE VALERA *being driven down the crowded street like a conquering hero, in an open car. The GPO still bearing the scars of 1916. British* SOLDIERS *and* RIC MEN *line the shop-fronts, impotent in the face of this public adulation.*

SMITH *stands among a phalanx of soldiers. He stares icily at* DE VALERA *through the cheering crowds.*

On the other side of the street BOLAND *and* COLLINS *stand, hidden in the sea of faces.*

BOLAND: God, he must hate it. So near, yet he can't touch him.

COLLINS: Don't worry, he'll try.

BOLAND: Not here—

COLLINS: No. But we can't let the long fella hang around . . .

87. INT. BEDROOM. DAWN

The bedroom of a working-class house. DE VALERA, COLLINS *and* BOLAND, *all sleeping on a bed in their crumpled suits.*

88. EXT. TERRACE. DAWN

A young boy runs full-tilt down the street. He raps on a window.

89. INT. BEDROOM. DAWN

COLLINS *sits bolt upright, instantly awake. He heaves* BOLAND *on to the floor.*

COLLINS: Get him out.

90. EXT. GARDEN. DAWN

COLLINS *and* BOLAND *and* DEV *run through the garden towards a laneway. There is a car waiting, engine running.* O'REILLY *stands by the open boot.*

91. EXT. TERRACE. DAWN

SMITH *and a group of* RIC MEN *pile out of a lorry. They begin to splinter the door with their boots.*

92. EXT. LANEWAY. DAY

DEV *is curled like a long spider in the boot.* COLLINS *salutes him.*

COLLINS: Remember something over there, Dev. You're my chief. Always—

[*He closes the boot as the car screeches off.*]

93. INT. HALLWAY. DAWN

A woman screaming on the stairway, a brood of kids behind her. The door gives way and SMITH *and his men pile in.* SMITH *backhands the woman, sending her tumbling to the floor.*

SMITH: Someone shut her up—

[*The* CHILDREN *wail. The* RIC MEN *begin to take the place apart.*]

94. EXT. GARDEN. DAY

The door is kicked open and SMITH *emerges. He runs out the garden to the laneway, which is quite empty.*

95. EXT. DAME STREET. DAY

SMITH, *returning from the raid, in foul humour, in an open-topped car. His driver turns a corner on to Dame Street and finds his passage blocked by a hackney driver trying to subdue a rearing horse.*

The driver beeps his horn repeatedly, tries to edge the car past. SMITH *stares balefully out his window. Then we hear the roar of a motorbike. He turns, sees—*

A goggled motorcyclist roaring towards him. From the sidecar another goggled youth pulls a Mauser pistol and shoots him many times.

96. INT. VAUGHAN'S. DAY

COLLINS *sits in a hotel room going through* BOLAND's *papers for America.* BOLAND *reads a paper, headlined with Smith's death.* COLLINS *holds out a passport.*

COLLINS: Passport. Your name's Harry Clyne. Until you get there.

[BOLAND *takes it.*]

COLLINS: I've had a birth cert done for you—and some bits and pieces.

[BOLAND *takes them, still saying nothing.* COLLINS *is upset.*]

COLLINS: Can't do without you, you know. I told him that.

BOLAND: Why does he want me?

COLLINS: He's afraid to leave the two of us together. We might achieve that republic he wants to talk to the world about.

[COLLINS *gets up.*]

COLLINS: They're filling up the Castle from Belfast. Things'll get rough, Harry. Rougher than we can imagine.

BOLAND: Don't let them near you, Mick.

COLLINS: They can't imagine a gunman in a pin-striped suit. On a bicycle. It's worked for us so far. So if my luck holds out and the wheels don't buckle . . .

[*He stops. He can't talk.* BOLAND *holds his arm.*]

BOLAND: Come to the train with me, Mick. Say hello to Kitty.

COLLINS: Kitty . . .

BOLAND: She'll need looking after while I'm gone . . .

97. INT. KINGSBRIDGE STATION. DAY

COLLINS, BOLAND *and* KITTY *walking through the crowded station.*

KITTY: He's leaving me, Mick.

COLLINS: Thought he was leaving me.

BOLAND: Shut up, the two of you. I'm leaving no one.

KITTY: Is it true, Mick, that all the women in America wear their skirts above the ankle?

COLLINS: Absolutely. Shameless hussies the lot of them.

BOLAND: There's a butterfly been seen in West Clare. Its wings are green, white and yellow. The lads see it as a sign.

[*They pass a posse of soldiers. Walk through them with hardly a glance.*]

COLLINS: Of course, you know the problem with butterflies.

KITTY: What's that?

COLLINS: They only last one day.

BOLAND: But what a day, Mick. What a day.

[*They have come to the station entrance. Crowds milling for the trains.*]

COLLINS: I'll leave yez here.

[*All three of them embrace.*]

BOLAND: It'll be all right, you know that—

COLLINS: I'm praying it will.

[*He turns away, overcome.*

BOLAND *walks on with* KITTY. *Turns one more time. Sees Collins is gone. Draws her on towards the train and its clouds of stream.*

BOLAND, *through the train window as it draws off.*

KITTY, *waving goodbye, enveloped by steam.*

KITTY *waves until the train is out of sight. Then walks slowly back.*

She is lost in thought, doesn't see a group of SOLDIERS *approaching her. She bumps into them.*]

SOLDIER: Your papers, miss.

[*She blanches, begins to fumble in her bag. Suddenly* COLLINS *appears from nowhere at her side.*]

COLLINS: Can a man not say goodbye to his wife in peace?

[*The* SOLDIER *backs off.* COLLINS *kisses* KITTY, *theatrically, under the* SOLDIER'*s gaze, until the* SOLDIERS *walk away.*]

COLLINS: Sorry.

KITTY: Where I come from we call that taking liberties.

COLLINS: I promised Harry to look after you . . .

[*He looks at her enigmatically. Then leads her rapidly the other way.*]

98. INT. CASTLE. DAY

MACBRIDE, *a huge bear of a detective from Belfast, strides through the Castle corridors, followed by three others, all from Belfast. They have come to put order in the Castle affairs, to replace the dead G-men.* BROY *and other* CASTLE FUNCTIONARIES, *follow them. They march into the record-room.*

MACBRIDE: Since you Dublin boyos can't sort out this Collins, I suppose it's up to us. You got his file?

BROY: Yes, sir.

[BROY *pulls out a drawer.* MACBRIDE *and his colleagues rifle through the files.*]

MACBRIDE: I want a list. Of anyone with a remote connection with this geezer. And I want them lifted—tonight.

BROY: You'll find it's not that simple, sir.

MACBRIDE: But it is simple, Mr. Broy. We'll make it that simple.

99. EXT. CASTLE COURTYARD. DAY

MACBRIDE *and the Belfast* DETECTIVES *leaving, talking to* BROY *and others at the doorway.*

MACBRIDE: There's a new regime in here and it's starting now.

[*He walks to the car, followed by his team. Gets inside.*]

MACBRIDE: A bit of Belfast efficiency is what they need.

[*The* DRIVER *starts the motor. The car blows up.*]

100. INT. CINEMA. DAY

Black and white newsreel footage, showing open-backed lorries crowded with the BLACK AND TANS *driving through Dublin streets, setting up road-blocks, searching through street markets, etc. A Pathé-style voiceover is heard.*

VOICE: They did not wait for the usual uniform. They came at once. They have looked death in the eyes in the Somme and Flanders and did not flinch. They will not flinch now. They will go on with the job—of restoring the rule of the King's law in Ireland . . .

101. EXT. DUBLIN TENEMENT. NIGHT

A Crossley tender full of BLACK AND TANS *is shooting up a tenement street. Again, the peacemakers are having a ball. Then from a street above, a kid lobs a petrol-bomb into the back of the lorry. The lorry explodes in flame.*

102. EXT. CASTLE. DAY

The Castle now is ringed with barbed wire, packed with BLACK AND TANS, *revolver-belts hanging low like gunslingers, armoured gun-carriages, machine-gun posts round the gates, a true fortress. An armoured carrier pulls through the gates and a group of about sixteen men emerge from it. These men are seriously tough. Efficient, with few words, from the British Secret Service. They stride into the building.*

103. INT. THE CASTLE. DAY

The new SECRET SERVICE MEN *swarm into the record-room, going through the files.* BROY *looks on, wearily.*

104. INT. THE CASTLE. DAY

A conference room. The British SS *around a table. Camera pans round their faces. Their commander,* SOAMES, *is handed files by* BROY.

SOAMES: What? Doesn't he have a face, this Collins? Doesn't he have corporeal form?

[BROY *hands him another file. A blurred photo on it, unrecognisable as Collins.*]

SOAMES: This is the best you've got?

BROY: Afraid so, sir.

SOAMES: Thank you, Boy. That will be all.

BROY: Broy, sir. Broy.

SOAMES: I am sorry.

[BROY *leaves*]

SOAMES: How do you catch a fish, gentlemen?

[MACCRAE, *one of the group, speaks up.*]

MACCRAE: Bait. A worm.

SOAMES: So we need to find bait for this Collins . . .

105. EXT. STRAND. DAY

COLLINS *and* BROY, *sitting on a sandbank by a railway track. A train whips by.*

COLLINS: I love trains, don't you, Ned?

BROY: What's so special about them?

COLLINS: They make me think of places I know I'll never see.

[*They stare at the sea for a moment. Then* BROY *speaks.*]

BROY: They're the elite of the British Secret Service. Churchill hand-picked them.

COLLINS: Give me everything you have.

[BROY *hands him a file.* COLLINS *flicks through it.*]

COLLINS: No addresses—

[BROY *shakes his head.*]

BROY: They keep to themselves.

COLLINS: They were sent here for one reason, weren't they?

BROY: To eliminate you and your boys.

[BROY *begins to shake, as if he's about to break down.*]

BROY: I can't hold on much longer, Mick. It's pulling me to ribbons—

COLLINS: Neither can I, Ned. But keep it a secret, will you?

106. EXT. SHELBOURNE HOTEL NIGHT.

SOAMES *walks out of the Shelbourne hotel, lighting a cigar. A passer-by asks him for a light. The match illuminates* COLLINS*'s face.* COLLINS *thanks him, walks on. He steps into a waiting car.* BROY *and* CULLEN *are inside.*

107. INT. CAR. NIGHT

CULLEN *drives.*

COLLINS: So that's Mr. Soames . . .

[BROY *nods.*]

COLLINS: How many to go, Ned?

BROY: Nineteen . . .

108. EXT. PARK. DAY

COLLINS *and* TOBIN *enter a park.* ROSIE, *a very young chamber-maid, sits there with* CHARLIE DALTON, *a young Volunteer. They could be lovers meeting for lunch.* DALTON *rises at* COLLINS's *approach.*

DALTON: This is Rosie, Mr. Collins.

[ROSIE *smiles and curtsies.*]

DALTON: Tell him about Mr. Soames, Rosie.

[ROSIE *is shy.*]

ROSIE: Well, he tips me every day. Not like some.

COLLINS: What time does he get up?

ROSIE: I come in at nine. He's washing, you see, behind the screen, so I don't see him. I empty the basket, take the linen. And then his hand comes over the screen with a half-crown in it.

DALTON: You shouldn't take it, Rosie.

ROSIE: But he's a gentleman, Charlie.

[COLLINS *smiles.*]

COLLINS: And you're a lady.

ROSIE: Thank you, Mr. Collins.

DALTON: Show him what you got from the basket, Rosie.

[ROSIE *smiles and takes a bundle from under her apron, hands it to* COLLINS.]

109. INT. CAR DAY

The car draws away from the park. BROY *and* CULLEN *in the back.* TOBIN *is driving.* COLLINS *is looking through the scraps of paper Rosie gave him.*

COLLINS: God bless, you, Rosie. We've got them.

110. INT. BACKSTAGE THEATRE. NIGHT

The whole of the SQUAD *stand around* COLLINS, *against the bizarre background of theatrical flats and props.*

COLLINS: These men have more experience than you ever will. You'll get one chance and one only. And I don't need to tell you how essential it is. So if anyone's not up to it, they have to say so now.

[COLLINS *waits for some of them to step down. No one moves, however.*]

COLLINS: Come on, lads. I know what some of you have been through. There's no shame in pulling out . . .

[*Again, there is no response.* COLLINS *seems about to cry.*]

COLLINS: Thank you. And nobody, tonight, stays in the usual places. Vaughan's, Crowe Street. If any of us are lifted, we're dead. Understood?

[*He turns abruptly away and makes for the door. Behind him,* CULLEN *pulls the grid away from the wall and begins to take out weapons.* COLLINS *walks from backstage into the empty auditorium.* O'REILLY *follows him.*]

O'REILLY: Mick, you said nobody stays at Vaughan's . . .

COLLINS: That's right, Joe.

O'REILLY: I got a message for you from Kitty.

COLLINS: Where is she?

O'REILLY: Vaughan's.

111. INT. VAUGHAN'S HOTEL. NIGHT

COLLINS *runs through the lobby, past the sleeping* BELLBOY *and takes the stairs two at a time.*

112. INT. VAUGHAN'S HOTEL ROOM. NIGHT

KITTY, *unpacking, getting ready for bed. The door bursts open and* COLLINS *comes through.*

COLLINS: Get your things, Kitty.

KITTY: Couldn't you say hello?

COLLINS: Hello.

[*He begins shoving her clothes into her case.*]

KITTY: Jesus, what do you think you're doing?

[*She grabs the case off him.* COLLINS *grips her with one arm, the case with the other.*]

COLLINS: Harry told me to look after you.

KITTY: And have you never heard of common courtesy?

COLLINS: No.

[*He pulls her towards the door. She slaps his face. It only makes him tighten his grip on her arm.*]

COLLINS: Please, Kitty, please, you can't stay here—

KITTY: Why?

COLLINS: Don't ask questions.

[*He drags her to the door again.*]

113. INT. VAUGHAN'S LOBBY. NIGHT

COLLINS *leads* KITTY *down the stairs. He kicks the* BELLBOY *awake.*

COLLINS: Johnny, Johnny—

[*The* BELLBOY *wakes.*]

COLLINS: Any of our boys comes in, tell them to stay somewhere else.

BELLBOY: Where else?

COLLINS: Anywhere.

[*He leads* KITTY *into the night.*]

114. INT. CASTLE—BROY'S ROOM. NIGHT

BROY *in his office, nervously filling a holdall with papers from his cabinet. He zips it shut and makes quietly for the door.*

115. EXT. CASTLE. NIGHT

BROY, *coming out of the door bumps into* SOAMES, *also leaving for the night, buttoning his greatcoat around him.*

SOAMES: Sufficient unto the day the evil thereof. Eh, Boy?

BROY: Yes, sir.

SOAMES: Or is it Broy?

BROY: Broy, sir. Goodnight, sir.

[BROY *walks off.* SOAMES *watches him go. He seems a lost, tiny figure. After a moment, an* SS MAN *in plain clothes emerges from behind the sentry-box.* SOAMES *nods at* BROY's *departing figure. The* SS MAN *follows.*]

116. INT. GRESHAM HOTEL. EVENING

COLLINS *leads* KITTY *through the crowded lobby of the Gresham Hotel, holding her by the elbow. There are a few officers and British military types around.*

KITTY: You're hurting me.

COLLINS: In here.

KITTY: (*Loudly*): I said you're hurting me.

[*A soldier glances around.* COLLINS *lets go of her arm. They could be two lovers, having a fight.* COLLINS *smiles at her. He holds out his arm for her to link with him.*]

COLLINS: Would that be better?

[KITTY *takes his arm. He draws her towards the stairs.*]

117 EXT. STREET—BROY'S HOUSE. NIGHT

BROY, *walking rapidly, carrying the holdall. He turns a corner, heading home, but sees a raid in progress outside his house.* BLACK AND TANS *circling the street outside, dragging lodgers from the interior.* BROY *rapidly turns back the way he came.*

   IN AN ALLEYWAY: *The* SS MAN *watching* BROY's *retreat, from deep in the shadows. After a time he follows.*

118. INT. GRESHAM HOTEL—BEDROOM NIGHT

COLLINS *is on the phone.* KITTY *sits in a chair, impatient.*

COLLINS: (*On phone*) Joe, I'm in the Gresham. Can't tell you why. No, it's fine. Call me if anything's up.

[*He replaces the telephone. Looks at* KITTY. *She is smiling.*]

KITTY: Tell him why.

COLLINS: Why what?

KITTY: Why you're in the Gresham. You're with a girl.

COLLINS: Harry's girl.

KITTY: Ah come off it, would you. I'm nobody's and you know that.

[*She stands and walks around the room.*]

KITTY: I mean the least you could do, Mick Collins, is make me feel at home.

[*She walks towards him and kisses him.*]

119. EXT. VAUGHAN'S HOTEL. NIGHT

BROY *outside the hotel. He hesitates a moment, then walks inside. The camera pulls back to reveal the* SS MAN, *watching. He notes down the address of Vaughan's.*

120. INT. VAUGHAN'S HOTEL. NIGHT

Camera follows BROY, *as he reaches the desk and checks himself in. The* BELLBOY *is once more asleep by the stairs.*

121. INT. GRESHAM HOTEL—BEDROOM. NIGHT

KITTY *withdraws from the kiss.* COLLINS *looks at her. Doesn't know what to do.*

KITTY: You do know how to give a girl a good time.

[COLLINS *turns in confusion and picks up the phone.*]

COLLINS: You want some tea?

122. INT. VAUGHAN'S—BROY'S BEDROOM. NIGHT

BROY, *in the tiny room, burning papers in the grate of the fire.*

123. INT. VAUGHAN'S. NIGHT

A group of BLACK AND TANS *enter the lobby. The* BELLBOY *finally wakes, swears under his breath.*

BELLBOY: Sweet mother of God—

124. INT. GRESHAM HOTEL—BEDROOM. NIGHT

A BELLBOY *brings tea.*

BELLBOY: Where will you have it, Mr. Grace?

COLLINS: Anywhere.

[*He signs the chit. As the* BELLBOY *leaves, he pours* KITTY *a cup of tea.*]

KITTY: Should I go, Mick?

COLLINS: You can't go, for Jaysus' sake. Why do you think I brought you here?

KITTY: I don't know. Why did you bring me?

COLLINS: Vaughan's isn't safe. Not tonight.

125. INT. VAUGHAN'S—BROY'S BEDROOM. NIGHT

The TANS *kick the door open and see* BROY, *sitting by the fire, holding the last burning sheaf in his hand. As they make for him, he throws it into the grate, watches it turn to ash. He looks at them, blinking, like a lost civil servant.*

TAN: What was on the paper, Paddy?

BROY: Words, just words.

[*One of the* TANS *whacks him with the butt of a rifle.*]

126. INT. GRESHAM HOTEL—BEDROOM. NIGHT

KITTY *looking at* COLLINS.

KITTY: What's happening tonight, Mick?

COLLINS: You don't want to know.

KITTY: Am I allowed to guess?

COLLINS: Have you heard from Harry?

KITTY: Yes, I've heard from Harry. He wrote. Harry always writes. When you both came to Granard the first time, you were the one I wanted. Yet Harry was the one who wrote. Why was that, Mick?

COLLINS: He's the marrying type—

KITTY: And you're not?

[COLLINS *looks at her, touches her cheek. Brings her face close to his. And kisses her.*]

127. INT. CASTLE. NIGHT

BROY *is dragged down the corridor towards an interrogation room.*

128. INT. GRESHAM HOTEL—BEDROOM. NIGHT

KITTY *draws back her head. She inhales deeply.*

COLLINS: Promise me something, Kitty.

KITTY: I'll promise you anything . . .

COLLINS: Promise me you'll never care about me.

KITTY: I promise . . .

   [*But she means the opposite. And Collins knows it.*]

129. INT. INTERROGATION-ROOM. NIGHT

The TANS *have strung a noose around* BROY'S *neck. It is hung from a pulley in the ceiling. They are smoking, matter-of-fact and bored.*

TAN: So, what was on that list?

   [BROY *says nothing. The* TAN *nods to his companion, who is holding the rope. His companion pulls the rope, lifting* BROY *into the air. Just when it seems he is gone, the* TAN *nods again and the rope is released.*]

TAN: You'd be surprised how long it takes to hang someone. We can go on all night. What was on it. Pat?

130. EXT. CITY. DAWN

Shots of TOBIN, CULLEN, DALTON *and other* VOLUNTEERS *cycling through the city streets, in groups of twos and threes. They could be early morning workers. A Mass bell tolls.*

131. INT. GRESHAM HOTEL. DAWN

The bell tolls round COLLINS *and* KITTY *in the opulent room. There are two single beds there. The dawn light comes through the window.*

KITTY: You've sent your boys out, haven't you?

COLLINS: How did you know?

KITTY: It's written on your face. Every step they take. Like so many valentines. Delivering bouquets.

132. EXT. HOTEL WINDOW. DAWN

Through a long, street level window, we can see the hotel guests having their breakfast. A MAN *walks swiftly into shot, a pickaxe handle in his hand. He swings it at the window and shatters it. The* GUESTS *stare through the falling glass. One of them rises, covering his eyes.* TOBIN, *standing on the pavement, shoots at him many times.*

133. INT. GRESHAM HOTEL—BEDROOM. DAWN

KITTY *draws* COLLINS *down on to the bed.*

KITTY: Do they deliver a love note, Mick? With the flowers?

　　[COLLINS *says nothing.*]

KITTY: What does it say?

134. INT. SHELBOURNE HOTEL—SOAMES'S BEDROOM. DAWN

SOAMES *stands half-dressed, shaving in front of a mirror. There is a knock on the door.*

SOAMES: Hang on, Rosie . . .

[*He steps behind a Chinese screen by the window. We hear the door opening.*]

SOAMES: Clean sheets, Rosie . . .

[*He shaves on, then notices there is no reply.*]

SOAMES: Rosie?

[*He drops the razor. Suddenly the screen is ripped apart with bullets. He is propelled backwards by the force of them, and crashes through the window into the street, below.*

The screen is kicked away by a young VOLUNTEER. *We can see the doorway behind him, the figure of young* CHARLIE DALTON *in it, holding* ROSIE *mute with a hand around her mouth. She pulls the hand free and emits one long hysterical scream.*]

135. INT. GRESHAM HOTEL—BEDROOM. DAWN

COLLINS: It says leave us be—

KITTY: Is that all? Not very romantic . . .

136. EXT. SQUARE. DAWN

A man does military exercises in the empty square. The roar of a motorbike is heard, and the same motorbike and side-car bounces down from the street into the square. The same goggled side-car passenger shoots at the officer, circling the square as he runs for a way out, allowing him no escape. Firing continually . . .

137. INT. GRESHAM HOTEL—BEDROOM. DAWN

COLLINS's *head is in* KITTY's *lap. She strokes his sweating forehead.*

COLLINS: You know what it says, Kitty. It says give us the

future. We've had enough of your past. Give us our country back. To live in. To grow in. To love.

138. INT. HOTEL ROOM. DAY

The WIFE *of an* SS MAN *gasps hysterically. Her* HUSBAND, *the* SS MAN, *is sitting on the bedside with her.*

HUSBAND: You could at least spare my wife this spectacle . . .

[*The* WOMAN *gasps.*]

WIFE: I'm . . . I'm . . .

[*We see a group of* VOLUNTEERS *stand above them, guns drawn. Their leader, a* SQUAD MEMBER, *nods to a* VOLUNTEER. *He takes the* WIFE *by the elbow and begins to lead her towards the door. The* SS MAN *uses the cover of her body to draw a gun and starts shooting. He takes down two* VOLUNTEERS, *until the* SQUAD MEMBER *finishes him off. The* WOMAN *screams, in a loud Dublin accent.*]

WOMAN: I'M NOT HIS BLEEDIN' WIFE . . .

139. INT. GRESHAM HOTEL—BEDROOM. DAWN

KITTY: Ah. So there's love there among the flowers. But what does it mean, Mick?

[COLLINS *whispers.*]

COLLINS: I don't know, Kitty.

KITTY: It means the opposite of hate, Mick.

[*She wraps herself around him.*]

140. INT. BOARDING-HOUSE. DAWN

Close on a young VOLUNTEER, *holding out a gun. His hand is shaking uncontrollably. We hear a voice.*

SS MAN: Just shoot straight this time.

> [*Cut to:*
> The SS MAN, *standing by the window. On a bed beside him, we see his companion, already dead.*
> The young VOLUNTEER *steadies his hand and shoots.*]

141. INT. GRESHAM HOTEL—BEDROOM. DAWN

COLLINS *looks into* KITTY's *eyes.*

COLLINS: Is it that simple?

KITTY: I would hope so.

> [*She kisses him. The sound of distant sirens can now be heard.* COLLINS *sits up suddenly.* KITTY *speaks quietly from the bed.*]

KITTY: So, Mick. Flowers delivered. Do you think they got the message?

142. EXT. CASTLE DAY

Utter mayhem, as the WIVES *and* FAMILIES *of British servicemen try to crowd in through the Castle gates, terrified now for their lives. A mass of cars packed with luggage, taxis,* SERVANTS *loaded down with cases and belongings, ambulances trying to get through the crush . . . The* GUARDS *at the gate try to put some order on the confusion . . .*

143. INT. DUBLIN WAREHOUSE. DAY

The members of the SQUAD, *gathered in an empty warehouse.* O'REILLY *tries to stem a bleeding wound on* CULLEN's *head.* CHARLIE

DALTON *dry retches into a sink.* TOBIN *stares into space. He seems to have aged twenty years.*

COLLINS *enters, like yet another member of the undead. He speaks softly.*

COLLINS: Any casualties?

[*There is a silence. Then* O'REILLY *speaks.*]

O'REILLY: Broy.

COLLINS: Broy wasn't out.

[*A terrible dread comes over him.*]

COLLINS: What do you mean, Joe?

O'REILLY: They lifted him in Vaughan's.

COLLINS: What was he doing in Vaughan's?

[O'REILLY *says nothing.*]

COLLINS: Oh sweet suffering Christ—poor Ned—

[*He slams himself against a wall.*]

144. EXT. CASTLE. DAY

The mayhem round the Castle gates is now like the US Embassy during the fall of Saigon.

Then through the hysterical mass, driving the other way, comes a Crossley tender, loaded with BLACK AND TANS. *It noses slowly through the chaos, out on to the street, then speeds away.*

145. EXT. CROKE PARK STADIUM. DAY

A Gaelic football stadium. People file through the gates, NEWSBOYS *sell papers carrying reports of the night's assassinations.*

146. EXT. STREETS. DAY

*The Crossley tender drives at a breakneck pace down Dame Street.
As it passes Trinity College, the body of* NED BROY *is thrown out of
it, naked and horribly maimed. The tender is joined by other troop
lorries, which tear recklessly through the Sunday streets.*

147. EXT. CROKE PARK STADIUM. DAY

*A hurling match begins. The crowd roars, with primitive vitality,
as the hurls clash and the ball flies through the air.*

148. EXT. CROKE PARK GATES. DAY

The TANS *sit with their guns between their knees, being thrown this
way and that as the tender whips through the north city slums. A
machine-gun is perched over the lorry's cabin, which swings wildly
with the lorry's movements. The slums they are moving through
give way to a large expanse of wasteland, with the concrete stadium
beyond it. The roar of the crowd can be heard from inside it. The
driver heads straight for the wooden doors of the stadium and
crashes through them, sending splintering wood flying everywhere.*

149. EXT. CROKE PARK STADIUM. DAY

*The game is in full flight, with the crowd engrossed in the speed
and excitement of it. At first nobody notices the tender, the lorries
behind it. But the tender drives at a slow, threatening pace right
into the centre of the field. The game gradually stops, and the roar
of the crowd dies down. The hurler in possession of the ball walks
towards the tender and whacks the ball towards it, so it bounces off
the metal radiator. The crowd laughs, and the hurler, catching
their mood, walks comically, clownishly, up to the tender, using
his hurl like a walking stick, making the crowd laugh once more.*

Then suddenly a shot rings out and he falls to the ground. The crowd still think he is clowning and laugh more. Till another shot rings out, then another. More players fall, and the others run in terror towards the stands. The crowd's laughter changes to panic. And the machine-gun on the tender begins to fire, raking the terraces, the field. The crowd stampedes in terror as the gunfire scythes through them. A priest staggers on to the pitch waving a white handkerchief, and is shot down in turn. And still the machine-gun on the tender rattles on, almost comically, till its ammunition is spent. Then the tender turns, weaves a circle through the field and drives back out of the shattered entrance, leaving the carnage behind it.

150. INT. CHURCH. DAY

A series of coffins are laid out in the nave of the church. Friends and relatives of the victims of the massacre line the way to pay their respects.

Camera tracks past coffin after coffin and finds COLLINS *and* O'REILLY *by the open casket in which lies the body of* NED BROY. COLLINS *is kneeling in prayer.*

O'REILLY taps COLLINS *on the shoulder. His head is bowed. He is praying.*

O'REILLY: Can't risk it any longer, Mick—

[O'REILLY *leads him away.*]

COLLINS: Who'll give in first, Joe? Us or them? The body or the lash?

151. EXT. PIER. DAY

COLLINS *stands at a pier at night. Fog drifts over the sea. A boat is being rowed towards him by two merchant seamen.* HARRY BOLAND *gets out, dressed in a garish American suit.*

COLLINS: You look like a gangster.

BOLAND: And you look like a ghost.

COLLINS: Welcome back, Harry.

[*They embrace.*]

BOLAND: How was it, Mick?

[COLLINS *says nothing.*]

BOLAND: You're famous over there now, Mick.

COLLINS: Over where?

BOLAND: America.

COLLINS: Ah. How was America?

[BOLAND *says nothing.*]

COLLINS: Dev didn't get to meet the President, did he? I never thought he would.

152. EXT. DUBLIN DOCKS. NIGHT

DE VALERA, *walking down the gangplank of a cargo ship.* O'REILLY *bundles him into a waiting car.*

O'REILLY: The Big Fella sends his regards . . .

[DEV *opens a newspaper. It has headlines about the continuing search for Collins.*]

DE VALERA: (*Softly*) We'll see who's the big fella . . .

153. INT. CATACOMBS. DAY

The cabinet is assembled. DE VALERA, BRUGHA, COLLINS, BOLAND, STACK, *etc. There is considerable tension in the air.*

COLLINS: Jesus, I feel like I've wandered into my own wake.

[DE VALERA *stands, majestically.*]

DE VALERA: We have had some communication from the British side. There is a slim possibility they might want to talk. But our tactics allow the British press to paint us as murderers. If we are to negotiate as a legitimate government, our armed forces must act like a legitimate army.

COLLINS: What exactly do you mean, Dev?

DE VALERA: I mean large-scale engagements . . .

COLLINS: You mean like in 1916. The great heroic ethic of failure. All marching in step towards slaughter. We might as well save them the bother and blow our own brains out.

BRUGHA: How dare you . . .

COLLINS: (*Shouting*) How do you think we've got them to this point? Where they'll even consider talking? We've brought them to their knees the only way we could. If you want us to play soldiers, they'll mow us down like cattle.

DE VALERA: They call us murderers.

COLLINS: War is murder. Sheer bloody murder. If you'd been here for the last year, you'd know that.

BRUGHA: Can the minister's remarks be put on record:

COLLINS: Yes.

DE VALERA: I propose an assault on the administrative centre of British rule in Ireland. The Customs House . . .

154. INT. THEATRE. DAY

COLLINS *is firing a tommy-gun at a wall full of theatrical flats. Quaint images of Ireland are blown to bits by the bullets.* BOLAND *and members of the Squad around him.*

COLLINS: Here we go, lads. The incredible new Thompson gun. Fresh from America. Like Dev's new tactics.

TOBIN: You mean he's serious.

COLLINS: Damn right he is. We march out in formation to face the biggest empire the world has ever seen. In broad daylight. We've as much chance as those cardboard dummies—

TOBIN: Why?

COLLINS: So we'll get better press. Can't you read the reviews, Harry? The Irish once more displayed their heroic aptitude for the role of martyr—

BOLAND: Stop it, Mick—

[COLLINS *stops shooting. Watches the dust settle.*]

COLLINS: You're right. I should do what I'm told.

[*He eyes the Squad.*]

COLLINS: I suppose we have to do it then.

[*They begin to arm up.*]

155. INT. WAREHOUSE. DAY

An open window looking out over the city. Grey ash is pouring through it from outside. CULLEN *stands there with* COLLINS. CULLEN, *who has been wounded in the arm, is tightening a bandage round the wound with his teeth. Through the scene, their faces turn grey with the ash.*

COLLINS: It's snowing.

CULLEN: No, it's the ashes from the Customs House files. Your birth certificate, maybe.

COLLINS: Some achievement, eh Tommy? Burning birth certs.

[BOLAND *enters.*]

COLLINS: How many did we lose?

BOLAND: Seventy-eight.

COLLINS: Jesus . . .

[*There are sudden sounds of feet, crashing doors from below.*]

COLLINS: Christ, not again.

CULLEN: There's files all over here.

COLLINS: Forget about them.

[*He places a tall chair under the skylight, and pulls himself up.* BOLAND *follows him. Below,* CULLEN *desperately tries to gather the files, his bandaged arm impeding him.*]

COLLINS: (*From above*) Leave them, Tommy, for Jesus' sake—

[*The footsteps of the Tans coming closer.* CULLEN *drops the files and clambers on the chair again, his wounded arm impeding him.* COLLINS *grabs him by the hand to pull him up, but* CULLEN *slips from his grasp and collapses on the floor, sending the chair spinning, among a mess of papers.*

COLLINS *goes to swing down to help him, but* BOLAND *grabs*

*him from above and swings him out of sight, slamming the
skylight shut.*

In the room, the door is kicked open. CULLEN *looks up as a
group of* TANS *enter.*

We see COLLINS *above, his face pressed against the glass.*
BOLAND, *again dragging him out of sight.*

In the room, the TANS *spreadeagle* CULLEN *against the wall.
An* SS MAN *gathers the papers.*

On the roof, COLLINS *struggles under the weight of* BOLAND,
who has his hand pressed over his mouth. BOLAND *whispers,
savage and fierce.*]

BOLAND: There's nothing you can do, Mick, do you hear
me?
Nothing—

[COLLINS's *face, struggling against* BOLAND's *hand. We hear the
sickening screams of Cullen as he is being roughed up below.
Every scream is echoed in the mute pain and fury on* COLLINS's
face. But for once, BOLAND's *grip is immovable.*

*We see a rope strung over the strut of the skylight. We hear
the scraping of a chair. We hear the sound of* CULLEN *praying,
then the chair is kicked. Silence.*

COLLINS's *face. Blood is flowing from* BOLAND's *hand.*

Sounds of the door opening, footsteps retreating once more.

BOLAND *removes his grip.*]

BOLAND: I'm sorry, Mick. Can't let them take you—

[COLLINS *turns his head, rises, looks down through the skylight.
We see* CULLEN *swinging from the rope below.*]

156. INT. HOUSE IN GREYSTONES. DAY

BOLAND *and* COLLINS *sit sipping tea with* DE VALERA *in a room that
looks out on the sea. A servant girl takes the tray away.*

COLLINS: So, how far are the British willing to go?

DE VALERA: That depends, Michael. How much longer we can hold out?

COLLINS: Four weeks. But keep it a secret.

DE VALERA: As little as that?

COLLINS: Unless you want us to use bows and arrows.

DE VALERA: Don't be flippant, Michael—

COLLINS: We lost near eighty men last week. You tell him, Harry—
[COLLINS *gets up and stands by the window, staring at the sea.*]

BOLAND: He's right, Dev . . .

157. EXT. ROAD BY SEA. DAY

COLLINS *and* BOLAND *cycling back from the meeting.*

COLLINS: I lied, Harry.

BOLAND: You what?

COLLINS: I doubt if we can hold out another week.

BOLAND: Do they know that?

COLLINS: Nobody knows.

BOLAND: But Dev's negotiating.

COLLINS: Yes. So he doesn't know either. And it's very important that he doesn't know, Harry. The world has to think we're invincible. Maybe then we can talk . . .

[*They cycle in silence for a moment*]

BOLAND: Kitty's down.

COLLINS: I heard.

BOLAND: Is she down to see you or me?

COLLINS: Maybe both of us, Harry.

[BOLAND *says nothing*.]

COLLINS: Take her down to Kingstown. Get some sea air.

BOLAND: You take her.

COLLINS: No, you do.

BOLAND: What do you say we both do?

158. EXT. KINGSTOWN PIER. DAY

KITTY *walks along the pier, flanked by* COLLINS *and* BOLAND.

KITTY: There was a horse called Irish Republic running at Donnybrook today.

BOLAND: What were the odds?

KITTY: Fifty to one.

[COLLINS *laughs*.]

COLLINS: Some odds.

BOLAND: There must be fifty thousand tommies here. Not two thousand of us. I'd say fifty to one is optimistic.

KITTY: Optimistic or no, she won.

[*She takes a bundle of notes from her pocket.*]

KITTY: Ten bob each way, that makes twenty-five pounds

plus the place money, seven pounds ten, and my stake makes thirty-three pounds ten shillin's thank you very much.

[*She links both of them.*]

KITTY: Why don't we let the Irish Republic buy us some dinner?

159. INT. RESTAURANT BY SEA. NIGHT

COLLINS, BOLAND *and* KITTY *after a sumptuous meal. Too much wine has been drunk. A bottle of whiskey is open on the table. A small orchestra is playing behind them and couples are dancing.*

KITTY: So, which one of you gunslingers is going to ask me to dance?

COLLINS/BOLAND: (*At the same time*) He will.

[*She flips a coin.*]

KITTY: Heads it's Harry. Tails it's Mick.

[*She reveals the coin. Heads.*
HARRY *rises, a lot of feeling in his face.*]

BOLAND: Kitty, dear—may I have the pleasure . . .

[*He leads her on to the floor and they dance.* HARRY *sweeps her round the floor, lithe and elegant.*
On HARRY *and* KITTY, *dancing.*]

BOLAND: I shouldn't have left, Kitty, should I?

KITTY: Why not?

BOLAND: I was a length ahead. Now it's more like neck and neck.

KITTY: It's not a race, Harry.

BOLAND: Ah. What is it then?

KITTY: You without him. Him without you. I can't imagine it.

BOLAND: A three-legged race . . .

KITTY: And anyone runs too fast, we'll all fall down.

[COLLINS *watches from the table. He drinks. We see from his face that he loves them both.*

　　Behind him we see a figure enter. It is JOE O'REILLY. *He is dishevelled, out of breath. He rushes up to* COLLINS*'s shoulder.*]

O'REILLY: Where the hell have you been, Mick?

COLLINS: For Jaysus' sake, Joe, would you give me one free night to be a human being—

O'REILLY: We've been combing the city for you. Have you heard?

COLLINS: No. And I don't want to hear. Would the bloody Irish Republic give me some time off—

O'REILLY: It's over.

COLLINS: Look, Joe, would you ever—

[*He stops. Turns.*]

COLLINS: What's over?

O'REILLY: It's over. They called a truce.

COLLINS: You mean it's finished? The whole damn thing?

O'REILLY: Yes.

COLLINS: You mean we've won? Lloyd George has thrown

in the towel? We've brought the British Empire to its knees?

O'REILLY: Yes.

COLLINS: Well, why the fuck didn't you say so, Joe?

[*He whoops and lifts* O'REILLY *off his feet and drags him on to the dance-floor.*]

COLLINS: It's over, Harry—

BOLAND: What's over?

COLLINS: You tell him—

[*He thrusts* O'REILLY *into* BOLAND'*s arms and sweeps around the floor with* KITTY.]

COLLINS: What was that horse called?

160. INT. MANSION HOUSE ROOM. DAY

A quite luxurious room, in marked contrast to their meetings before. DE VALERA, COLLINS, BOLAND, BRUGHA, STACK—*a session of the cabinet.* COLLINS *is agitated, furious.*

COLLINS: No. I won't do it. I'm not a politician. I won't go to London.

BRUGHA: You're the strongest card we have.

COLLINS: They call me an assassin and a murderer, for Jaysus' sake. Can you even see Churchill shaking my hand?

DE VALERA: We've broached it with them. We've had no objections.

COLLINS: You're the statesman, Dev. You're the one they

know. You've had some sense of how far we can push them.

DE VALERA: Yes. Perhaps that's the problem . . .

COLLINS: Don't do this to me, Dev. Don't do it. I'm no good at talk. I'm a yob from West Cork, Dev, please—

DE VALERA: You'll head our team, Michael. To negotiate a treaty, for the first time in history, between Ireland and England. We need to keep a final arbiter in reserve.

COLLINS: And that'll be you?

DE VALERA: That will be the Irish people. And me as the president of the Irish Republic.

[COLLINS *shakes his head disbelievingly.*]

161. INT. MANSION HOUSE. CORRIDOR. DAY

COLLINS *walks in with* BOLAND, *followed by the ever faithful* O'REILLY.

COLLINS: Why does he want me there, Harry?

BOLAND: You're a hero.

COLLINS: Save me the bullshit—

BOLAND: You heard him. You're the strongest card we have.

COLLINS: Can I believe him?

BOLAND: You have to.

COLLINS: I've one simple asset. All these years. No one knows who I am.

162. EXT. MANSION HOUSE. DAY

They emerge through doors to the street outside and are suddenly surrounded by journalists and photographers.

JOURNALISTS: We want a statement, gentlemen. Which one of you is Michael Collins?

[COLLINS *points to* O'REILLY.]

COLLINS: He is.

[COLLINS *ducks through the mêlée, leaving the diminutive* O'REILLY *to cope with the journalists, and walks towards* KITTY.]

163. EXT. DAWSON STREET. DAY

The street packed, shoulder to shoulder, with cheering people. KITTY, BOLAND *and* COLLINS *walking down it, arm in arm. They get separated by the crush of the crowd. They shout at each other words we can't hear, as their hands reach out towards each other, but the crowds press them further apart. We end on* COLLINS's *face, straining to grasp his two friends, his eyes strangely troubled, panic-stricken . . .*
Fade to black.

164. INT. HOTEL ROOM. DAY

The lounge of a hotel suite. On KITTY's *face, as she reads a letter from Mick.*

KITTY: 'I wish to God someone else was in this position and not I. They couldn't defeat us by force of arms but now I swear they're trying to defeat us by force of verbiage. The English language was never meant to be spoken like that. How in God's name did these people ever get to run an Empire?'

[*A hand reaches down and touches her neck. The camera pulls back and reveals* HARRY.]

KITTY: Don't Harry.

[*He moves around as if to kiss her. She turns away.*]

KITTY: Harry—please . . .

HARRY: Why not?

KITTY: Because you'll get hurt.

[*She looks at him and says very directly.*]

KITTY: I'm in love with him.

[*He is cut to the bone.*]

KITTY: I'm sorry, Harry. But I had to tell you.

HARRY: Have you told him?

KITTY: No. And maybe I never will. He made me promise, you see. Never to care for him. But I do. I know that since he went away. And I'm only telling you because I can't hurt you.

[*He touches her face.*]

HARRY: Lucky Mick.

165. EXT. DECK OF BOAT. DAY

A newspaper photograph of Collins and the other signatories signing the Treaty. A wind whips the paper. We pull back to see COLLINS, *reading the paper on the deck of a boat over the Irish Sea.*

His voice, over.

COLLINS: [*Voiceover*] 'Dear Kitty,
Today I signed my own death-warrant. And I thought, how strange, how ridiculous, a bullet could have done it just as easily four years ago . . .'

166. EXT. DUBLIN BAY. MORNING

We see COLLINS*'s point of view.*
Dublin Bay, coming out of the morning mists. It looks strangely restful, for a country that is about to be torn apart by civil war . . .

167. EXT. DOCKS. DAY

COLLINS *pushes his way through a mass of photographers to a waiting car. He steps inside.*

168. INT. CAR. DAY

Inside sits HARRY BOLAND, *the same paper on his knees. The car pulls off.*

BOLAND: Is it true, Mick?

[COLLINS *speaks softly.*]

COLLINS: It's the best anyone could have got, Harry.

BOLAND: Partition. And an oath of allegiance . . .

COLLINS: They can't give us the Republic. It's not within their comprehension. And that's why Dev sent me, Harry.

BOLAND: What do you mean, Mick?

COLLINS: He knew they wouldn't give us it. That's why he sent me. He wanted someone else to bring back the bad news.

[COLLINS *can't look at* BOLAND. *But we see tears are streaming down* BOLAND'*s face.*]

COLLINS: We'll have an Irish Free State. A government of our own. And we can use it to achieve whatever republic we want. It's either this or war. And I won't go to war over a form of words . . .

BOLAND: What if it's war either way, Mick?

COLLINS: Don't ever say that again, Harry—

169. INT. SHELBOURNE HOTEL. DAY

KITTY *in the crowded lobby. We see the car pull up.* BOLAND *gets out, waves at* KITTY *briefly and walks on.* COLLINS *tries to pull him back, but* BOLAND *won't have it.* COLLINS *enters the lobby.*

KITTY: What's wrong with Harry?

[COLLINS *is now fighting back the tears.*]

COLLINS: He's read the papers.

170. INT. HOTEL RESTAURANT. NIGHT

COLLINS *sitting with* KITTY *in morose silence.*

KITTY: Say something, would you?

[COLLINS *says nothing.*]

KITTY: I've known the two of you for four years. You've lived together, slept together, fought together. But your war's over now.

COLLINS: What if it's only beginning?

KITTY: Christ, I'd be better off back in Leitrim—

[*She stands up and walks off.*]

COLLINS: Kitty—

[*He follows her into the lobby. There he meets* O'REILLY.]

O'REILLY: Dev wants to meet you, Mick—

171. INT. GOVERNMENT OFFICES. NIGHT

Lavish, splendid rooms, a total contrast to their previous environments. COLLINS *stands alone with* DE VALERA.

DE VALERA: You published the terms without my agreement . . .

COLLINS: They were the best we could get.

DE VALERA: In your opinion . . .

COLLINS: And what's more, Dev—you sent me there because you knew they were the best we could get.

DE VALERA: That's idle speculation.

COLLINS: No. It's the truth. Otherwise you would have gone yourself.

[DE VALERA *says nothing, but his silence says it all. He avoids* COLLINS'*s eyes.*]

COLLINS: I know it doesn't give us the Republic, Dev. But it gives us freedom to achieve the Republic. Peacefully. And surely it's time for peace.

[*He takes a breath.*]

COLLINS: When I agreed to go, you told me we could negotiate on behalf of the Dail and the Irish people. If they
reject it, I'll reject it. But if they stand by it I'll stand by
it. And I want to know that you'll do the same.

[DE VALERA *says nothing.*]

172. INT. SHELBOURNE HOTEL. NIGHT

COLLINS *sleeping. The door opens and* KITTY *enters.*

KITTY: All right, you've won. Damn you.

[*She walks towards him.*]

KITTY: Do you always win, Mr. Collins?

[COLLINS *holds out an arm to her.*]

COLLINS: Rarely, Miss Kiernan. Very rarely.

[*She crawls into bed beside him.*]

KITTY: Jesus, I hate you.

[COLLINS *holds her close. He says softly.*]

COLLINS: Join the club . . .

173. INT. NATIONAL UNIVERSITY. DAY

COLLINS *walking, followed by* O'REILLY *and a mass of reporters.
Down a long corridor. The longer he walks the more crowded it
becomes. Questions being plied on him—about the treaty,* DE VAL-
ERA'S *opposition, a potential split . . . He answers none of them.*
     *There is a hubbub from the doors ahead. They are opened by a
flunkey.* COLLINS *walks into the Dail meeting. The visitor's Gallery
is packed and the debate raging.*

COLLINS *walks down the steps, through the delegates, ignoring every stare like a boxer entering a ring. He takes his seat beside* ARTHUR GRIFFITH, *gazing at the speaker.*

DE VALERA *has the floor.*

DE VALERA: We were elected by the Irish people, and did the Irish people think we were liars when we said we meant to uphold the Republic?

[ARTHUR GRIFFITH *rises.*]

GRIFFITH: In the letters that preceded the negotiations not once was the demand made for recognition of the Irish Republic. If it had been made we knew it would have been refused—

[CATHAL BRUGHA *leaps to his feet.*]

BRUGHA: So Mr. Collins is asking us to accept an oath of allegiance to a foreign king, and the partition of the northeast corner of the country?

GRIFFITH: The boundary commission will make the North unworkable. Mr. Collins—the man who won the recent war—will ensure that it does. He has himself described the Treaty as a stepping-stone towards the ultimate freedom—

BRUGHA: The chairman of the delegates, Mr. Griffith, has referred to Mr. Collins as the man who won the war—

VOICES: Hear hear . . .

[COLLINS *rises to his feet.*]

COLLINS: On a point of order—are we discussing the Treaty or discussing myself—

BRUGHA: The minister does not like what I have to say—

COLLINS: Anything that can be said about me, say it—

BRUGHA: Mr. Collins' position in the army was as head of one of the subsections. None of the staff sought notoriety except him—

VOICE: He never fired a shot for Ireland—

COLLINS: Come on, Cathal, out with it—

BRUGHA: One person was selected by the press to put him in a position he never held. He was made a romantic figure, a mystical character which he certainly is not. The person I refer to is Michael Collins.

[ARTHUR GRIFFITH *rises.*]

GRIFFITH: He was the man whose matchless energy and indomitable will carried Ireland through the terrible crisis. He was the man who fought the Black and Tans until England was forced to offer terms. And if my name is to go down in history I want it associated with the name of Michael Collins.

[*Griffith's words have the desired effect. A majority of the delegates rise to their feet, cheering.* COLLINS *rises and tries to quell them. The anti-Treatyites begin to create mayhem.*]

COLLINS: I would plead with every person here. Make me a scapegoat if you will, call me a traitor if you will, but please save the country. The alternative to this treaty is a war which nobody in this gathering wants to contemplate. If the price of freedom, the price of peace, is the blackening of my name, I'll gladly pay it.

174. INT. DAIL CHAMBERS. DAY

COLLINS, *sitting in the same position, hours later. Absolute silence. The votes are being counted.* COLLINS *looks across at* BOLAND *who is* sitting close to DE VALERA. BOLAND *looks away. The* SPEAKER *enters. He bangs the gavel.*

SPEAKER: A majority of seven in favour of the Treaty . . .

[*And suddenly the place erupts. Shouting across the benches. Punches thrown, chairs flung . . . until* DE VALERA*'s shrill voice makes itself heard above the babble.*]

DE VALERA: As a protest against the ratification of this Treaty which is bound to subvert the Republic, I and my deputies are going to leave this house.

[*He walks towards the door. The other anti-Treatyites follow him.* COLLINS *rises, like a mad animal . . .*]

COLLINS: DEV!

[DE VALERA *walks on, without hesitation.* COLLINS *stands, and has to watch as comrade after comrade follow* DE VALERA *out the door—*BRUGHA, STACK, CHILDERS, TOM BARRY, DAN BREEN, *some members of the Dublin Squad—all men he has fought with, worked with.* BOLAND *is the last to rise to his feet and leave.*]

COLLINS: Not you, Harry—

[*They stare at each other across the benches. Tears in both men's eyes. Then* BOLAND *turns abruptly away and leaves.*]

175. INT. DAIL. DAY

Silence, in the half-empty chamber. The deputies remaining cannot believe what has happened. COLLINS *sits alone, with his head in his hands. After what seems an age, he raises his face.*

COLLINS: Let's get down to it, then. We've got a country to run . . .

176. EXT. DUBLIN CASTLE. DAY

In the Castle grounds, the British VICE-CONSUL *stands, dressed in ceremonial feathered hat, ceremonial sword, etc. Lines of soldiers stand round him, as if waiting for a ceremony that might never take place. They seem to have been waiting for some time. There is a* SQUADDY *with his hand on the rope of the British flag, a group of trumpeters, everyone waiting patiently in the freezing cold. The* VICE-CONSUL *glances at the large clock and away again. Then into the grounds sweeps a line of cars.* COLLINS *steps out,* TOBIN *and other* OFFICERS *behind him.* COLLINS *stares round at the assemblage. Looks up at the whipping British flag. Then walks towards the* VICE-CONSUL.

VICE-CONSUL: You are seven minutes late, Mr. Collins.

COLLINS: You've kept us waiting seven hundred years. You can have the seven minutes.

> [*The* VICE-CONSUL *is taken aback.* COLLINS *stares round the line of soldiers.*]

COLLINS: Let's get this over with.

> [MACREADY *steps back, rigid and frozen now. He turns to his Commanding Officer, who gives the signal to the buglers. They play the 'Last Post' as the British flag is lowered. A strange, empty ceremonial air to it all, highlighting the pathos of what everyone fought over. Afterwards,* COLLINS *looks at the wrapped-up flag. He turns to* MACREADY.]

COLLINS: So that's what caused all the bother . . .

> [*He looks at the Vice-Consul and smiles grimly.*]

COLLINS: And now? Do I get to wear that hat?

177. EXT. SQUARE. COUNTRY TOWN

DE VALERA *speaking to a large crowd.*

DE VALERA: This Treaty bars the way to Independence with the blood of fellow Irishmen. And if it is only by civil war we can get our independence, so be it. The Volunteers may have to wade through Irish blood, through the blood of some members of the government, in order to get Irish Freedom . . .

178. EXT. COUNTRY ROAD BY GRANARD. DAY

COLLINS *is driven along a country road,* MCKEOIN *beside him. The road is lined with trees and each tree bears a poster, with* COLLINS*'s face on it.*

COLLINS: When did you last see Harry?

MCKEOIN: Three weeks ago.

COLLINS: If it came to an open fight, what would he do?

MCKEOIN: He'd lose.

[COLLINS *stares at him.*]

MCKEOIN: They'd all lose. And they know it. Because they know you.

[COLLINS *says softly.*]

COLLINS: I couldn't do it, Sean . . .

[*The car turns and they see Granard approaching. There is a plume of smoke rising from the square. As the car draws nearer, we can see it is the platform and the bunting burning.*]

MCKEOIN: Someone got here first.

179. EXT. SQUARE. EVENING

COLLINS *speaks from the smouldering platform to the crowded square.*

COLLINS: The Treaty that was signed in London may not give us the ultimate freedom, but it gives us the freedom to achieve the ultimate freedom . . .

[*Shouts and cries are heard at the back of the crowd. Then a gunshot. The crowd runs this way and that—and through it comes a horse, charging, terrified of the noise behind it—then another, and another—a mass of them, driven by Republican youths at the end of the square. A rock flies through the air and hits* COLLINS *on the forehead.*

    Then suddenly a fusillade of shots is heard behind him. COLLINS *turns and sees* KITTY *on the platform behind him, emptying a Thompson gun into the sky. The crowd falls silent, shocked.*]

KITTY: Now let the man speak.

[*She hands the gun back to* MCKEOIN. COLLINS *is gobsmacked. She winks. He turns back to the podium.*]

COLLINS: The Treaty may not give us a Republic, but it gives us the freedom to achieve the Republic . . .

180. INT. GRANARD HOTEL. NIGHT

KITTY *bathes* COLLINS*'s bleeding forehead in a basin of water.*

COLLINS: God, you put the heart across me, Kitty.

KITTY: I like the sound of your voice, Mick. It's that simple. If anyone tried to silence it, I'd kill them.

[*She raises his head from the basin.*]

KITTY: Does this remind you of something?

COLLINS: The day we met.

KITTY: You, me and Harry.

[COLLINS *sings softly*.]

COLLINS: For it will not be long, love, till our wedding day . . .'

KITTY: They won't accept the Treaty, Mick, no matter how the vote goes. You heard what De Valera said.

COLLINS: That they'll wade through rivers of blood—

KITTY: Whose blood do you think he's talking about?

[COLLINS *says nothing*.]

KITTY: Yours, Mick.

181. EXT. FOUR COURTS. DAY

A newsboy selling papers. The headlines proclaim the massive vote in favour of the Treaty. Bewigged barristers come and go.

A series of cars screech up. Armed Republicans pour out of the cars, push through the barristers and begin to occupy the courts.

182. EXT. FOUR COURTS. DAY

COLLINS, O'REILLY *and* TOBIN *drive towards the Four Courts.*
COLLINS *steps out of the car and strides towards the Four Courts entrance. As he reaches them, a group of young* VOLUNTEERS *step out and block his way.* COLLINS *grabs the* VOLUNTEER *facing him and lifts him off the ground*

COLLINS: Who gave you that, you guttersnipe?

[*He wrenches the gun from him, throws it on the ground behind him. The other* VOLUNTEERS *are pale, afraid to move. Then* COLLINS *sees a figure walking down the steps towards him. It is* ERNIE O'MALLEY.]

COLLINS: What's this about, Ernie?

O'MALLEY: We've taken over the Four Courts, Mick.

COLLINS: You bloody fool . . .

O'MALLEY: Mind your language.

COLLINS: Come on, you idiot. Do you want to start a civil war—

O'MALLEY: We'll defend the Republic.

COLLINS: Forget the Republic. These kids have never seen a gun before . . .

[*He gestures to the youths barring his way.*]

O'MALLEY: We know how to train them . . .

COLLINS: The way I trained you?

[O'MALLEY *doesn't reply.*]

COLLINS: Where did you get your orders?

O'MALLEY: From the Volunteer executive.

COLLINS: Ah. You mean Dev's half of it?

[COLLINS *abruptly turns away. He re-enters the car with* O'REILLY *and* TOBIN. *He sits there for a moment, staring at the scene he has left.*]

COLLINS: (*to* TOBIN) You know what this means, Liam.

TOBIN: We could split down the middle . . .

[*He gestures to the driver to move off.*]

183. INT. HOTEL ROOM. NIGHT

KITTY *enters the room, her coat and hat on. She goes to turn on the light.*

COLLINS: Leave it off, Kitty.

[*She turns to see* MICK, *sitting on a sofa in the darkness.*]

KITTY: Why?

COLLINS: There's a gunman out there by the railings.

[*She strides rapidly to the large window and pulls open the curtains, standing in full view of the window.*]

COLLINS: *Kitty!*

[*He leaps off the sofa.*]

KITTY: They won't shoot me, Mick. And do you know why?

[*He reaches her and pulls her out of view. As he does so, a bullet crashes through the windows, missing them both.*]

COLLINS: For the love of Jesus, Kitty—

KITTY: They can't shoot us, Mick. It's not possible. Because I'm going to live to see you old.

[*He smiles.*]

COLLINS: How old?

KITTY: Old enough to see your hair grey.

COLLINS: I come from a long line of baldies.

KITTY: Bald then. I can live with that.

[*She kisses him.*]

184. INT. GOVERNMENT OFFICES. DAY

COLLINS *sits with* GRIFFITH, COSGRAVE *and other members of the Provisional Government.* COLLINS *is demented.*

COLLINS: I will not fight against men I trained, I fought with—

COSGRAVE: The people have spoken, Mr. Collins. Overwhelmingly, for the Treaty you brought home.

GRIFFITH: They've occupied the Four Courts, half of O'Connell Street, Limerick, Cork. It's anarchy out there.

COLLINS: Better anarchy than civil war.

GRIFFITH: Churchill has offered us artillery—

COLLINS: Let Churchill do his own dirty work.

GRIFFITH: Maybe he will, Michael. Maybe he will . . .

185. EXT. FOUR COURTS. NIGHT

Republican sentries stand on the Four Courts roof, like Indians out of a Western.

186. EXT. O'CONNELL STREET. NIGHT

COLLINS *driving down it with* MCKEOIN *and* O'REILLY. *He sees the windows opposite the GPO are sandbagged. Armed figures inside.*

COLLINS: Churchill has offered us British artillery. Could you bear to use it, Joe?

O'REILLY: I do what I'm told, Mick.

[COLLINS *notices something.*]

COLLINS: Stop the car—

MCKEOIN: It's not safe, Mick—don't—

COLLINS: Do what you're told, Joe—

[O'REILLY *jams on the breaks.* COLLINS *darts out, follows a retreating figure.*]

187. INT. VAUGHAN'S HOTEL—BEDROOM. NIGHT

BOLAND, *making his way up the stairs.*

COLLINS: Harry . . .

[BOLAND *turns.*]

COLLINS: Talk to me, Harry . . .

BOLAND: I don't want any bullshit, Mick—

COLLINS: I don't either.

[*A kid with a pistol underneath the stairs recognises him. He stands, his eyes wide.*]

BOLAND: Come upstairs.

[*He turns and* COLLINS *follows him.*]

COLLINS: The old kip's just the same . . .

BOLAND: Not quite . . .

COLLINS: Still full of gunmen, only now they're aimed at me.

BOLAND: Not yet, Mick . . .

188. INT. BEDROOM. NIGHT

BOLAND's *things all over the room.* COLLINS *stands there, when he enters. He suddenly seems immensely tired.*

BOLAND: Is it true what I heard? You're engaged to Kitty?

[COLLINS *is abstracted. He glances up and sees a photograph of* KITTY *on the wall.*]

COLLINS: Should I apologise for that too?

BOLAND: No. I'm happy for you both.

COLLINS: You don't look it.

BOLAND: Maybe I don't, Mick. But I'm trying. I miss the way it used to be.

[COLLINS *looks at him fondly.*]

COLLINS: They say you're Dev's right-hand man now, Harry.

BOLAND: I suppose that's how it goes.

COLLINS: We were too dangerous together. But you know the funny thing, Harry? For the first time I'm scared.

[BOLAND *laughs.*]

BOLAND: The Big Fella scared? Don't give me that.

COLLINS: You told me once how good I was at bloody mayhem. How I left the Brits in the halfpenny place. And that's what I'm scared of. Once it starts, there'll be no stopping me.

BOLAND: Don't let it start then. Tear up that Treaty.

COLLINS: It's the only thing we've got—

BOLAND: So then. It starts. We fight.

[COLLINS *grips* BOLAND's *head close to his, like a woman's.*]

COLLINS: No. They fight.

BOLAND: Just go, Mick, will you—

COLLINS: We don't, Harry—

[COLLINS *reaches for him once more.* BOLAND *screams, with sudden fury.*]

BOLAND: *I SAID GO!*

[COLLINS *stares at him ashen-faced. After a beat the door kicks open and the kid from downstairs stands with a gun in his hand.*]

COLLINS: Do it, kid, it'd save a lot of bother—

[BOLAND *knocks the gun from the kid's hand.* COLLINS *goes.*]

189. EXT. FOUR COURTS. DAWN

A large gun fires from the street beside the Four Courts. The shell explodes on the brickwork, throwing debris everywhere. COLLINS *stands with the other officers behind the gun.* O'REILLY *is next to him.*

COLLINS: How would you like a new boss?

[*The gun fires again and again.* COLLINS *turns and walks away. The sound of the gun firing seems to reverberate through him. He keeps walking, as if he cannot stand to see what is happening. Each successive explosion is etched on his face.*]

190. EXT. O'CONNELL STREET. DAY

Sporadic firing all up and down the street. The FREE STATE TROOPS *move from sandbagged posts into doorways, pushing forwards all the time.*

191. EXT. HAMMAN HOTEL. EVENING

The hotel is blazing. Republicans pour out of the front doorway, hands over their heads. A pause, as the last one exits. Then a lone figure walks forward, out of the smoke. It is BRUGHA. *He has two guns, blazing. One of the* FREE STATE OFFICERS *calls out.*

OFFICER: Cathal . . .

> [BRUGHA *fires at him, wounding him in the arm. A young* GUNNER *fires into* BRUGHA *then, repeatedly. The* OFFICER *screams at the* GUNNER, *who keeps on firing, until the* OFFICER *silences him with a blow from his own gun.*
>
> *The* OFFICER *walks forward then, holding his wounded arm.* BRUGHA *is lying on the steps, quite dead.*]

192. INT. GOVERNMENT BUILDINGS. NIGHT

COLLINS *with* O'REILLY, MCKEOIN *and other* FREE STATE OFFICERS. *Maps of Dublin and the countryside pinned to the walls.*

COLLINS: I want those units that cleaned up O'Connell Street in Limerick by tomorrow morning—

> [*The* OFFICER *with the wounded arm enters.*]

OFFICER: They got Brugha, Mick.

COLLINS: You mean Cathal . . .

OFFICER: Yes.

COLLINS: Then say so.

> [*He turns back to the map, without expression.*]

COLLINS: Then we take Cork city, from the sea. They won't know what hit them. Poor bastards . . .

193. EXT. O'CONNELL STREET. NIGHT

O'REILLY *drives* COLLINS *through the smoking ruins of O'Connell Street. Dead and wounded are being taken from the buildings. The car stops by an ambulance.*

COLLINS: Ask them is there any sign of Harry—

[O'REILLY *gets out, as* COLLINS *grimly surveys the wreckage around him.*
O'REILLY *talks to an officer, then walks back.*]

O'REILLY: A bunch of them shot their way through to the docks, heading for the catacombs. He thinks Harry was with them—

COLLINS: Get word through, Joe. He's not to be touched.

O'REILLY: How can I get word through? They've blown up all the power lines—

COLLINS: Then drive like fuck, would you—

194. INT. CATACOMBS. NIGHT

BOLAND *running through the ground floor. The windows are suddenly ablaze with light, as lorries circle outside.*

195. EXT. CATACOMBS. NIGHT

FREE STATE SOLDIERS *spilling from the lorries.*

196. INT. CATACOMBS. NIGHT

BOLAND *comes to a metal grid in the floor. He lifts it and sees piled wooden barrels below. He inches his way down and pulls the grid back over.*

197. INT CAR. NIGHT

O'REILLY, *frenetically driving* COLLINS *through the north side of the city.*

198. INT. CATACOMBS. NIGHT

BOLAND, *inching his way along the barrels. He can hear footsteps, as the Free Staters comb the place above. He freezes, looks up and sees—*
    BOLAND's *point of view—*
    the metal grille. Several pairs of boots walk across it. BOLAND *holds his breath. Then he hears an agonising creaking sound, as the triangular wedge holding the barrels in place gives way.*
    Above the grille:
    Two FREE STATERS *stop, hearing the sound.*
    Below the grille:
    BOLAND *gritting his teeth. Suddenly the barrels begin to roll beneath him.*
    An explosion of gunfire suddenly comes from above, through the grille, punching holes in the rolling barrels, Guinness foaming everywhere. BOLAND *is hit in the shoulder. He staggers to his feet and runs through the vaults.*

199. INT. CAR. NIGHT

O'REILLY *driving through the docklands.*

200. INT. CATACOMBS. NIGHT

BOLAND, *running through the huge underground vaults of the catacombs.* FREE STATE SOLDIERS *chasing him, firing from the hip.* BOLAND *ducks behind a pillar as the gunfire peppers it with holes. He ducks his way from pillar to pillar, avoiding the repeated burst of automatic fire, then tumbles through an arch at the end of the vault.*

201. TUNNEL BELOW LIFFEY. NIGHT

BOLAND *staggers and splashes his way through a huge, dripping tunnel underneath the river Liffey. It is a black hole, the only light coming from the entrance, way behind him. He feels his way along the dripping walls till he reaches the aperture of a sluice-pipe, several feet above the floor. He pulls himself up with his last strength, and crawls inside.*

Behind him, the FREE STATE TROOPS *find their way into the tunnel. They walk into the inky blackness, guns at the ready, silhouetted by the light behind them.*

In the sluice, BOLAND *inches his way forwards with his elbows. He hears the splashing feet approach him and freezes, craning his head under his elbows to look back. He can see the* FREE STATERS, *inching their way through the pitch-black tunnel. They pass the sluice-pipe, without noticing him.*

BOLAND *crawls on.*

202. EXT. SLUICE-PIPE. NIGHT

BOLAND, *reaching the exit of the sluice-pipe. He can see the Liffey waters, lapping several feet below him. He eases his way into the water and begins to swim painfully off.*

A cigarette falls in the water beside him and sizzles. BOLAND *turns in the water, looks up and sees . . .*

203. EXT. LIFFEY WALL. NIGHT

A young FREE STATER *looking down, exhaling cigarette-smoke. The* FREE STATER *smiles. Then fires.*

204. INT. CAR. NIGHT

O'REILLY *blares his horn and crashes through a roadblock.* FREE STATERS *stare at the retreating car.* COLLINS *in the back can hear the sound of gunfire.*

205. EXT. LIFFEY WALL. NIGHT

The young FREE STATER *still firing. Then his ammunition clip runs out.*

　We see BOLAND's *dead body bobbing below him, blood seeping through to the Liffey waters.*

206. EXT. CATACOMBS. NIGHT

O'REILLY *screeches to a halt by the catacombs. Soldiers all around run towards them, guns drawn..*

O'REILLY: Calm down, would yez. It's the Big Fella—

　[COLLINS *gets out of the car. He walks to the edge of the Liffey wall. He sees two* FREE STATERS *dragging* BOLAND's *dead body up and from the water. He walks slowly forwards towards them, as they lay the body on the ground. He bends over it, lifts up* BOLAND's *bloodied face.*

　　COLLINS *closes the eyelids.*]

COLLINS: (*Softly*) What happened? Who closed your eyes?

　[*The Young* FREE STATER *steps forwards.*]

FREE STATER: He was trying to make it across the river, sir. I saw him and plugged him from above.

COLLINS: I didn't ask you.

FREE STATER: Who did you ask?

[COLLINS *rises in sudden fury and drags him towards the edge.*]

COLLINS: I asked him—

FREE STATER: But he's dead, sir—

COLLINS: And you killed him, you little uniformed git—

[COLLINS *dangles him over the water's edge.*]

COLLINS: You plugged him, you little Free State shit—you were meant to protect him—

FREE STATER: He was one of them, sir.

[COLLINS *suddenly drops him in the water, twenty feet below. He watches him splash and struggle.*]

COLLINS: No, sonny. You don't understand. He was one of us.

207. EXT. SHELBOURNE HOTEL. DAY

KITTY *alights from a cab and makes for the hotel doors. She is wearing a hat with a fringe of black lace.*
O'REILLY *emerges from the front doors of the hotel.*

KITTY: Is he up there?

O'REILLY: He's been there all day, miss.

208. INT. HOTEL ROOM. DAY

KITTY *enters. The room is in darkness, the curtains are closed.* COLLINS *speaks from the shadows.*

COLLINS: The papers said his last words were 'Have they got Mick Collins yet?'

KITTY: It's not true, Mick, you know it can't be . . .

COLLINS: I don't know anything any more . . .

KITTY: Every time you both went off somewhere he'd say:
'Don't worry, Kit, Mick will be all right.' And it used to
cheer me up so he'd say, 'There you go, Kit. I'm the one
knows how to make you happy.'

[*She breaks down.* COLLINS *holds her.*]

COLLINS: He wasn't made for all this.

KITTY: And you were?

COLLINS: If I could get them to talk, Kitty, just talk . . .

209. INT. PUBLIC HOUSE. NIGHT

O'REILLY *sits with three* REPUBLICANS, *almost in the same way as
the old days, except that* COLLINS *is now absent. It is very late at
night.*

O'REILLY: Tell Dev that Mick wants to talk. Nothing more,
nothing less.

REPUBLICAN: Not in Dublin.

O'REILLY: Where, then?

REPUBLICAN: West Cork, there might be a chance.

O'REILLY: He'd never get out of there alive.

REPUBLICAN: Sure, doesn't he come from there?

O'REILLY: It's like bandit country—

REPUBLICAN: They're bandits he trained, then.

O'REILLY: Maybe. But he doesn't know the new boys.

REPUBLICAN: He'll have to get to know them . . .

210. EXT. PUBLIC HOUSE. DAWN

O'REILLY *walks down the empty street, away from the pub. The* REPUBLICANS *stand in the doorway, observing him go. Dawn is coming up over the city.*

211. INT. GOVERNMENT OFFICES. DAWN

O'REILLY *comes into* COLLINS*'s office. He finds him asleep over the desk. He shakes him awake.*

COLLINS: What time is it?

O'REILLY: Seven. Have you been here all night?

[COLLINS *rubs his eyes. He looks ashen.*]

COLLINS: Any news?

O'REILLY: They say if you went to Cork, there'd be a possibility.

COLLINS: What do you think?

O'REILLY: We've cleared them out of everywhere but West Cork. Thornton was shot up there last week.

COLLINS: You think my own countrymen would kill me?

[O'REILLY *says nothing.*]

COLLINS: How would you like a new boss, Joe? Or did I ask you that already?

O'REILLY: You'd be crazy to go, Mick . . .

[COLLINS *rises, goes to the window and stares outside.*]

COLLINS: So. I'm crazy. Get a convoy ready, Joe.

212. EXT. GOVERNMENT BUILDINGS. DAY

A convoy of vehicles waiting. COLLINS *walks down the steps in his military greatcoat. He stumbles and begins coughing violently.* O'REILLY *runs down from behind to help him.*

COLLINS: Just give me some of your cough mixture, Joe—

[O'REILLY *takes a small noggin out of his pocket.* COLLINS *drinks from it, then makes for the cars.*

O'REILLY *watches him go with a look of doom in his eyes. Then he runs after him, leaps in beside* COLLINS.]

213. INT. DRIVING CAR. DAY

COLLINS, *sitting in the back seat with* O'REILLY.

COLLINS: Who invited you along, Joe?

O'REILLY: If you're going down I'm going with you.

COLLINS: Down where, Joe? West Cork?

214. EXT. COUNTRYSIDE. DAY

COLLINS'*s convoy speeds through the countryside. An armoured car in front, a car with a machine-gunner behind.*

215. EXT. WOODFIELD. EVENING

With the burnt remains of COLLINS'*s family home in the foreground, we see the convoy drive past.*

216. INT. CAR. EVENING

COLLINS *and* O'REILLY, *driving past.*

COLLINS: This is where it all started, Joe. Fenian stories by the fireside.

O'REILLY: That's your home?

COLLINS: Was. Till the Tans burnt it.

217. INT. JAMES SANTRY'S FORGE. EVENING

Old JAMES SANTRY, *shoeing a horse. Collins's convoy pulls up in the background.* SANTRY *turns, as* COLLINS *and* O'REILLY *approach.*

SANTRY: In the name of God, what are you doing here, Mick?

COLLINS: Haven't I a civil war to run?

[COLLINS *embraces him.*]

SANTRY: Mick, the countryside's rotten with Irregulars—

COLLINS: But how many of them was born here, James?

[*He turns to* O'REILLY.]

COLLINS: Joe, meet James Santry. Taught me everything I know. Maybe he wishes he hadn't—

[COLLINS *kisses* SANTRY *before he has a chance to reply.*]

COLLINS: Now, how about a pint of Clonakilty Wrastler?

218. EXT. FOUR-ALLS PUB. EVENING

COLLINS, O'REILLY *and* SANTRY *make their way towards a tiny pub in the fading light. Behind them the convoy of vehicles follows, at a crawl. The* MACHINE-GUNNER *eyes nervously the low hedges and stone walls.*

SANTRY: You're a bloody sitting duck, man. Tell him.

O'REILLY: I've told him. He's a sitting duck.

COLLINS: How else would they know I'm here, Joe?

219. INT. FOUR-ALLS PUB. NIGHT

A group of men drinking inside. When COLLINS *enters they turn and eye him.* COLLINS *walks to the bar.* SANTRY *and* O'REILLY *follow behind.*
    One DRINKER *mutters.*

DRINKER: Come to flog us that treaty, have you?

COLLINS: I'm flogging fuck-all. I've come to buy. Drinks for the fucking county on me.

220. EXT. FOUR-ALLS PUB. NIGHT

The convoy, sitting outside in the moonlight. The GUNNER *still eyes the fields around. Locals are pouring into the pub.*
    Some ragged YOUNG MEN *with rifles are observing the scene. One of them turns and runs into the night.*

221. INT. FOUR-ALLS PUB. NIGHT

COLLINS, *in the centre of the now crowded pub. He and* JAMES SANTRY *are reciting 'Skibbereen', exchanging alternate verses.*

COLLINS: 'They set my roof on fire with their cursed English spleen.

And that's another reason why I left old Skibbereen.'

[*The crowd roars its approval.*]

222. EXT. SMALL COTTAGE. NIGHT

A tiny cottage in a mountainous area. The YOUTH *runs towards it.*

223. INT. SMALL COTTAGE. NIGHT

DE VALERA, *sitting by a fire alone. He is shivering, his eyes burning. The* YOUTH *enters.*

DE VALERA: Is it him?

YOUTH: Looks like it. Looks like he wants to meet—

DE VALERA: Doesn't he know it's out of my hands?

YOUTH: Whose hands is it in then, Chief?

[DE VALERA *mutters to himself.*]

DE VALERA: You should have listened to me, Michael. You heard but you didn't listen . . .

YOUTH: Listened to what?

DE VALERA: So can I trust him?

YOUTH: Can you trust anyone these days, Chief?

[DEV *looks up like a hunted animal. The* YOUTH *smiles. There is no knowing what his smile means.*]

224. INT. FOUR-ALLS PUB. NIGHT

COLLINS *continues with the ballad.*

COLLINS: And that's another reason why I left old Skibbereen . . .

[COLLINS*'s voice has sunk low, however. The pub door opens,
and the same ragged* YOUTH *comes in. He whispers something
to* O'REILLY. O'REILLY *draws him outside.* COLLINS *makes his
way through the crowd to the door.*]

225. EXT. FOUR-ALLS PUB. NIGHT

O'REILLY, *talking to the* YOUTH. COLLINS *bursts through the door.*

COLLINS: Say it to me, kid—

[*The* YOUTH *turns.*]

YOUTH: And who the fuck are you?

COLLINS: I'm the fucking idiot that asked to meet Dev.

YOUTH: And who's Dev when he's at home?

[*The* YOUTH *smiles again. A killer smile, with no remorse.*]

YOUTH: But if I did know this Dev, what would you have to
say to him?

[COLLINS *grabs the* YOUTH *by the lapels, lifts him bodily off the
ground.*]

COLLINS: Tell him that Harry Boland's death was enough.
Tell him Mick Collins wants to end this bloody mayhem.

[*The camera jumps back—to a hayrick in the fields. A figure
is standing in the darkness. It is* DE VALERA. COLLINS*'s voice
drifts through, clearly.*]

COLLINS: Tell him I'm sorry I didn't bring back a republic.
But nobody could have. He was always my chief. I
would have followed him to hell if he'd asked me. And
maybe I did.

[*He releases the* YOUTH.]

COLLINS: But it's not worth fighting for. Any more. We've got to learn to live.

[COLLINS *turns away.*]

COLLINS: *You tell him that.*

[*The* YOUTH *calls back.*]

YOUTH: And where can he reach you?

COLLINS: Here.

[*He kicks the door open and walks inside.*]

226. EXT. HAYRICK. NIGHT

The smiling YOUTH *walks over to* DE VALERA. DE VALERA *is shaking uncontrollably.*

DE VALERA: Oh God help us . . .

YOUTH: So I take it you heard?

DE VALERA: Oh Jesus, Mick, God forgive me, Harry—

[*The* YOUTH *smiles. He seems to be enjoying Dev's nervous breakdown.*]

YOUTH: Have you any reply?

[DEV *walks off into the night like a lost soul.*]

YOUTH: He's come all this way. Be kind of rude not to give him an answer . . .

[*The* YOUTH *stands until* DEV *has vanished into the night. Then he turns and walks slowly back to the pub.*]

227. INT. FOUR-ALLS PUB. NIGHT

The pub is now emptying. COLLINS *is drinking at the bar with*
O'REILLY *and* JAMES SANTRY.
      The YOUTH *enters by the back door. He sidles up to* COLLINS.

YOUTH: He says he'll meet you tomorrow.

COLLINS: What's wrong with now?

YOUTH: His nerves are at him.

      [COLLINS *drinks.*]

YOUTH: Beal Na Blath. There's a farmhouse to the left on
      the Bandon side. Around twelve.

COLLINS: And what's your name, kid?

YOUTH: I'm just the messenger.

      [*The* YOUTH *goes.*]

228. EXT. DUBLIN STREET. DAY

A car drives KITTY *through the Dublin streets. She has a hatbox in
her hand. The car stops outside a clothes shop, with an elaborate
wedding display in the window.* KITTY *steps out, and looks at the
display.*

229. EXT. ROADWAY. DAY

COLLINS's *convoy drives through the morning mists. He smiles
wryly.*

COLLINS: Should I ask the whole bunch to the wedding,
      Joe? Do you think that would fix it?

O'REILLY: Be a big bloody wedding, Mick.

COLLINS: Ask the whole country. Call it marital diplomacy. Dev as best man. Lloyd George and Churchill as the bridesmaids.

[O'REILLY *laughs.*]

230. INT. DUBLIN SHOP. DAY

KITTY *stands in a lift, which brings her to an upper floor. She walks into a large room in which various mannequins display different styles of wedding dress. A woman walks towards her.*

231. EXT. LONG'S PUB. DAY

COLLINS*'s convoy pulls up outside a small isolated country pub. There is a* MAN *at the door.*

O'REILLY: Beal Na Blath?

[*The* MAN *points towards the west with one hand. The other hand is inside the swing-doors of the pub. As the convoy draws slowly off.*
We cut to . . .]

232. INT. LONG'S PUB. DAY

The MAN*'s hidden hand is clutching a rifle. At the bar sits the smiling* YOUTH, *with several others. They grab rifles and rush out the back door.*
A lone OLD MAN *by the bar mutters.*

OLD MAN: Collins has gone west but he won't go east . . .

233. INT. DUBLIN SHOP. DAY

KITTY *sits on a chair. An assistant takes a wedding dress out of a box and holds it up to her.* KITTY *shakes her head.*

234. EXT. BEAL NA BLATH HEIGHTS. DAY

An ambush is already in place, above the tiny road. Six or eight men crouched behind hedges. The others from the pub are running furiously towards them.

235. INT. DRIVING CAR. DAY

The car slows down slightly. COLLINS *looks up.*

COLLINS: Why are you stopping?

DRIVER: Something up ahead.

[*The car turns a corner and is blocked by an overturned cart. Suddenly the car is raked with gunfire.* O'REILLY *grabs the* DRIVER'*s shoulders.*]

O'REILLY: Drive like hell . . .

COLLINS: *Don't—*

[*There is a strange insistence in his voice.* O'REILLY *screams.*]

O'REILLY: Ram the fucking thing.

[*The* DRIVER *puts the boot down and smashes into the cart but can't shift it.*
    The vehicles behind skid to a halt, all over the roadway. Gunfire is now peppering them from all directions.
    COLLINS *snatches up a rifle, swings out of the car.*]

COLLINS: It's the end of the road, Joe—

[*He rolls on to the road. He returns fire from under cover of the open door.*
    A group of sheep scurry from the sides of the road. One of them is riddled with bullets.]

236. INT. DUBLIN SHOP. DAY

There are now numerous dresses, all strewn around KITTY. *The assistant unwraps yet another one from its box, holds it up for* KITTY. KITTY *stands and walks forward, holds it against herself, looks at herself in a large mirror.*

237. EXT. COUNTRY ROAD. DAY

COLLINS *on the ground firing.* O'REILLY *screams at the gun-carriage behind him.*

O'REILLY: Get that thing firing, would you.

> [*The machine-gun is jammed, however.* O'REILLY *somersaults out of the back of the car and jumps into it, throwing the gunner to one side. He jerks the gun belt to free it and pulls the trigger. Swathes of lead begin to cut through the hedges beyond.*]

238. EXT. BEAL NA BLATH HEIGHTS. DAY

The machine-gunfire rakes the hedges like a scythe. The ambush party dives to the dirt to avoid it.

239. EXT. BEAL NA BLATH ROADSIDE. DAY

O'REILLY'S *covering fire is ferocious.* COLLINS *pulls two pistols from his belt and stands, firing both simultaneously.*

240. EXT. BEAL NA BLATH HEIGHTS. DAY

The smiling YOUTH, *crouched behind a gnarled tree with a fork. He takes aim and fires one shot.*

241. EXT. BEAL NA BLATH ROADSIDE. DAY

COLLINS *jerks backwards and falls on the road.*

O'REILLY *keeps up the covering fire, staring towards the hillside. He glimpses fleeing figures, then fires a few rounds after them. Then gradually, silence descends. He laughs with relief, fires off a few more rounds.*

O'REILLY: Close one, eh, Mick? Thought they could get the Big Fella—

[*There was no reply. He turns. Sees* COLLINS *lying on the roadside, a pool of blood around his head.*]

O'REILLY: Oh Jesus, Mick—talk to me—

[*He tumbles off the vehicle and runs to* COLLINS. *He gathers him in his arms. There is a gaping wound in the side of* COL-LINS's *head.*]

O'REILLY: Say something, Mick, would you? Don't fucking go on me . . .

242. INT. DUBLIN SHOP. DAY

KITTY, *struggling into the dress she has chosen. The assistant drapes an elaborate veil over her face.*

243. INT. HOTEL CORRIDOR. NIGHT

KITTY, *returning from the wedding shop. She is carrying the clothes and hat-boxes of her wedding trousseau. She turns a corner and finds herself face to face with a* FREE STATE SOLDIER *lounging opposite a hotel doorway. When their glances meet he stands to attention.*

She stares at him. And she knows, instantly, the news he is bringing her.

She screams—NO!!!

She drops the boxes. He reaches out to her and her hands flail out at him in an anguish of grief. She turns and runs down the corridor, kicking the boxes aside.

244. INT. DARK ROOM. DAY

JOE O'REILLY, *talking towards the camera the way he did at the beginning of the film.*

JOE: That's why he died, Kitty. He knew the risks he was taking when he went down there. But he thought them worth taking. He took them for us, Kitty. For every gobshite in this country. No matter what side they were on.

[*We see* KITTY. *She is lying on a bed as if she's been lying there for days. The curtains are drawn to shut out the daylight.*]

JOE: And if he saw you now, do you know what he'd say, Kitty?

[*He walks to the curtains and pulls them. Light floods the room.*]

JOE: Get up off the parliamentary side of your arse and get a bit of colour in your face.

[KITTY *smiles in spite of herself.*]

KITTY: But he would have said it much better, Joe . . .

JOE: No regrets, Kit. That's what he'd say.

[*She takes his hand and rises to her feet. She embraces him.*]